Foreign Direct Investment (FDI) and Financial Integration

By

Abhijit Bhattacharya
Assistant Professor of Economics,
Pingla Thana Mahavidyalaya,
Paschim Medinipur,
West Bengal

New Century Publications
New Delhi, India

New Century Publications,
74, Ansari Road, Ground Floor,
Daryaganj, New Delhi – 110 002 (India)

Tel.: 011- 4358 7398, 4101 7798, 2324 7798
E-mail: info@newcenturypublications.com

www.newcenturypublications.com

Editorial office:
4800/24, Ansari Road,
Daryaganj, New Delhi – 110 002

Tel.: 98117 88655

First Published: **July 2021**

ISBN: **978-81-7708-525-9**

Published by New Century Publications and printed at Milan Enterprises, New Delhi

Designs: Patch Creative Unit, New Delhi

PRINTED IN INDIA

About the Book

Foreign investment, an important source of non-debt finance, is a subject of topical interest. Countries of the world, particularly developing economies, are vying with each other to attract foreign capital to boost their domestic rates of investment and also to acquire new technology and managerial skills. Intense competition is taking place among the fund-starved less developed countries to lure foreign investors by offering repatriation facilities, tax concessions and other incentives.

The beginning of the 21st century has already marked a tremendous growth of international investments, trade and financial transactions along with the integration and openness of international markets.

Investment in a country by individuals and organisations from other countries may take the form of direct investment (creation of productive facilities) or portfolio investment (acquisition of securities). Foreign direct investment (FDI) is the outcome of the mutual interests of multinational firms and host countries. The essence of FDI is the transmission to the host country of a package of capital, managerial skills and technical knowledge. FDI is generally a form of long-term international capital movement, made for the purpose of productive activity and accompanied by the intention of managerial control or participation in the management of a foreign firm.

FDI is usually contrasted with portfolio investment which does not seek management control, but is motivated by profit. Portfolio investment occurs when individual investors invest, mostly through stockbrokers, in stocks of foreign companies in foreign land in search of profit opportunities.

FDI is widely considered superior over other forms of capital inflows for achieving sustainable development. Developing countries are strongly advised to rely primarily on FDI, in order to supplement national savings by capital inflows and promote economic development.

FDI is not an unmixed blessing. When foreign investment is

competitive with home investment, profits of domestic industries fall, leading to shrinkage of domestic savings. Foreign firms stimulate inappropriate consumption patterns through excessive advertising and monopolistic/oligopolistic market power. Similarly, foreign firms are able to extract sizeable economic and political concessions from competing governments of developing countries. Consequently, private profits of these companies may exceed social benefits.

Thus, governments in developing countries have to be very careful while deciding the magnitude, pattern and conditions of private foreign investment. The key question is how host countries can minimise possible negative effects and maximise positive effects of FDI through appropriate policies.

This book attempts to explain and statistically examine the various dimensions of FDI with reference to India. It also includes chapters on portfolio investment, financial integration, international investment position (IIP) of South Asian countries and international financial integration of high income European Union (EU) countries.

About the Author

Dr. Abhijit Bhattacharya is currently Assistant Professor of Economics, Pingla Thana Mahavidyalaya, Paschim Medinipur, West Bengal. He holds M.A., M.Phil., and Ph.D. degrees in Economics. He successfully completed a research project on Global Financial Crisis funded by the University Grants Commission (UGC), New Delhi. He has contributed articles in journals and chapters in various books edited by eminent scholars. He has attended and presented papers at international and national level conferences and seminars. One of his collaborative research papers on FDI was adjudged the best at the International Accounting, Finance, Economics and Banking Conference held at Flame University, Pune during December 17-18, 2017.

Contents

Preface

The wave of liberalization and globalization sweeping across the world has opened many national markets for international business. Global private investment, in most part, is now made by multinational corporations (MNCs). Clearly, these transnational organizations play a major role in world trade and investments because of their demonstrated management skills, technology, financial resources and related advantages. The beginning of the 21st century has already marked a tremendous growth of international investments, trade and financial transactions along with the integration and openness of international markets.

Hence, foreign investment is a subject of topical interest. Countries of the world, particularly developing economies, are vying with each other to attract foreign capital to boost their domestic rates of investment and also to acquire new technology and managerial skills. Intense competition is taking place among the fund-starved less developed countries to lure foreign investors by offering repatriation facilities, tax concessions and other incentives.

Investment in a country by individuals and organisations from other countries may take the form of direct investment (creation of productive facilities) or portfolio investment (acquisition of securities). Direct investment or more appropriately foreign direct investment (FDI) is the outcome of the mutual interests of multinational firms and host countries. The essence of FDI is the transmission to the host country of a package of capital, managerial skills and technical knowledge. FDI is generally a form of long-term international capital movement, made for the purpose of productive activity and accompanied by the intention of managerial control or participation in the management of a foreign firm.

FDI is usually contrasted with portfolio investment which does not seek management control, but is motivated by profit. Portfolio investment occurs when individual investors invest, mostly through stockbrokers, in stocks of foreign companies in foreign land in search of profit opportunities.

However, the distinction between FDI and portfolio investment is not watertight because sometimes FDI policy and portfolio investments are intertwined.

FDI is widely considered superior over other forms of capital inflows for achieving sustainable development. Developing countries are strongly advised to rely primarily on FDI, in order to supplement national savings by capital inflows and promote economic development. Three major types of FDI are typically differentiated: resource-seeking FDI, market-seeking FDI and efficiency-seeking FDI.

Resource-seeking FDI is motivated by the availability of natural resources in host countries. This type of FDI is historically important and remains a relevant source of FDI for various developing countries.

Size and growth of host country's markets are among the most important FDI determinants. Traditionally, FDI has been the only reasonable means to penetrate local markets in various developing countries. Many developing countries have liberalized their import regime, thereby enabling MNCs to choose between exporting or undertaking FDI. Geographically dispersed manufacturing, slicing up the value chain and the combination of markets and resources through FDI and trade are becoming major characteristics of the world economy.

Efficiency-seeking FDI, i.e. FDI motivated by creating new sources of competitiveness for firms and strengthening existing ones, may then emerge as the most important type of FDI. Accordingly, the competition for FDI would be based increasingly on cost differences between locations, the quality of infrastructure and business-related services, the ease of doing business and the availability of skills. Obviously, this scenario involves major challenges for developing countries, ranging from human capital formation to the provision of business-related services such as efficient communication and distribution systems.

FDI is not an unmixed blessing. Governments in developing

countries have to be very careful while deciding the magnitude, pattern and conditions of private foreign investment.

When foreign investment is competitive with home investment, profits in domestic industries fall, leading to a fall in domestic savings. Foreign firms stimulate inappropriate consumption patterns through excessive advertising and monopolistic market power. Similarly, foreign firms are able to extract sizeable economic and political concessions from competing governments of developing countries. Consequently, private profits of these companies may exceed social benefits.

Furthermore, foreign firms may influence political decisions in developing countries. In view of their large size and power, national sovereignty and control over economic policies may be jeopardised. In extreme cases, they (foreign firms) may bribe public officials at the highest levels to secure undue favours. Similarly, they may contribute to friendly political parties and subvert the political process of the host country.

Thus, foreign investment is not an unmixed blessing. Governments in developing countries have to be very careful while deciding the magnitude, pattern and conditions of private foreign investment.

Therefore, the key question is how host countries can minimise possible negative effects and maximise positive effects of FDI through appropriate policies.

Financial integration is a key element in the transmission process and hence for the smooth conduct of monetary policy. Financial integration also leads to a better diversification of risks and makes a positive contribution to financial stability by improving the capacity of economies to absorb shocks. Fully integrated financial markets also pave the way for shocks to propagate more quickly among market participants, which could necessitate appropriate safeguards. To mitigate the risks and maximise benefits from financial integration, it is imperative that the financial markets are developed further. Enhanced co-operation among various regulatory authorities is also important for ensuring effective corrective action in an increasingly integrated environment. Moreover, it is necessary to establish further linkages amongst the various components of financial infrastructure—the trading, payment, clearing, settlement and custodian systems.

Financial integration encompasses a complex interplay of various factors such as policy initiatives, structure and growth of financial intermediaries, organic linkages among market participants and the preference of savers and investors for financial instruments. The study of financial integration must keep in view the heterogeneity of markets, dimensions of integration, measurement issues and perceived benefits and risks of integration.

Financial integration at the theoretical level has been postulated in several ways. The most popular economic principles of financial integration include the law of one price, term structure of interest rates, parity conditions such as purchasing power parity, covered and uncovered interest parity conditions, capital asset price model and arbitrage price theory.

Broadly, financial integration occurs in three dimensions, viz. nationally, regionally and globally. From an alternative perspective, financial integration could take place horizontally and vertically. In the horizontal integration, inter-linkages occur among domestic financial market segments, while vertical integration occurs between domestic markets, regional and international financial markets.

Paschim Medinipur **Abhijit Bhattacharya**

1

Foreign Direct Investment (FDI): Theoretical Settings

Foreign investment is a subject of topical interest. Countries of the world, particularly developing economies, are vying with each other to attract foreign capital to boost their domestic rates of investment and also to acquire new technology and managerial skills. Intense competition is taking place among the fund-starved less developed countries to lure foreign investors by offering repatriation facilities, tax concessions and other incentives. However, foreign investment is not an unmixed blessing. Governments in developing countries have to be very careful while deciding the magnitude, pattern and conditions of private foreign investment.

Liberalisation and globalization wave sweeping across the world has opened many national markets for international business. Global private investment, in most part, is now made by multinational corporations (MNCs) also referred to as transnational corporations (TNCs). Clearly, these transnational organisations play a major role in world trade and investments because of their demonstrated management skills, technology, financial resources and related advantages. Recent developments in the global market are indicative of the rapidly growing international business. The beginning of the 21st century has already marked a tremendous growth of international investments, trade and financial transactions along with the integration and openness of international markets.

1.1 Globalization and Cross-border Investments

The 1990s witnessed a paradigm shift towards market-oriented economic policies and a careful dismantling of obstacles in its wake. Globalization has resulted in the creation of a new business framework.

1.1.1 Meaning and Impact of Globalization: Globalization implies widening and deepening integration with the *globe*, i.e. with people and processes abroad. The trend towards the evolution of a global society is generally thought of in economic terms and in terms of the consequences of the revolution in communication technologies. There is undoubtedly much greater economic integration among the nations of the world today. Globalization is widely seen as the most important factor that could influence economies of nations the world over in the new millennium. The rapid advancement in information technology and communications has made it not just possible but absolutely essential for economies of the world to adapt or fall by the wayside. More changes can be expected in the business scenario specifically in terms of openness and adaptiveness.

1.1.2 Transnational Corporations: Globalization has resulted in the growing concentration and monopolisation of economic resources and power by transnational corporations and by global financial firms and funds. This process has been termed transnationalisation, in which fewer and fewer transnational corporations are gaining a large and rapidly increasing proportion of world economic resources, production and market shares. Where a multinational company used to dominate the market of a single product, a big transnational company (TNC) now typically produces or trades in an increasing multitude of products, services and sectors. Through mergers and acquisitions, fewer and fewer of these TNCs now control a larger and larger share of the global market, whether in commodities, manufactures or services.

1.1.3 Globalization of National Policies: Globalization process has led to globalization of national policies and policy-making mechanism. National policies (including economic, social, cultural and technological) that until recently were determined by the States and people within a country have increasingly come under the influence of international agencies and processes or by big private corporations and economic/financial players. This has led to the narrowed ability of governments and people to make choices from options in economic, social and cultural policies.

Most developing countries have seen their independent policy-making mechanism capacity eroded, and have to adopt policies influenced by other entities, which may on balance be detrimental to the countries concerned. The developed countries, where the major economic players reside, and which also control the processes and policies of international economic agencies, are better able to maintain control over their own national policies as well as determine the policies and practices of international institutions and the global system. However, it is also true that the large corporations have taken over a large part of decision-making even in the developed countries, at the expense of the power of the state or political and social leaders.

1.1.4 Flexible Production Processes: Globalization of the economies across the world has changed the notions of manufacturing, productivity and competitiveness. Flexible production processes and structures are being increasingly put in place to compete in very dynamic markets where product life is very short and discerning customers with higher purchasing power and more differentiated and international tastes are demanding much more product variety, higher quality and greater value for money. The new production systems are increasingly moving to the network form of enterprises, each contributing to the production and distribution according to their respective core competencies. Therefore, competitiveness now requires the ability to constantly take the most advantageous position or niche in the rapidly changing market environment.

1.1.5 Globalization and Developing Countries: The issue that concerns developing countries is how they can ensure greater participation of the weaker economies in the global process and what needs to be done to ensure that the course of globalization benefits more people in more countries. The uneven and unequal nature of the present globalization is manifested in the fast growing gap between the rich and poor people of the world and between developed and developing countries; and by the large differences among nations in the distribution of gains and losses.

This imbalance leads to polarisation between countries and groups that gain, and the many countries and groups in society that lose out or are marginalised. Globalization, polarisation, wealth concentration and marginalisation are therefore linked through the same process. In this process, investment resources, growth and modern technology are focused on a few countries, mainly in North America, Europe, Japan and a few East Asian countries. A majority of developing countries are excluded from the process, or are participating in it in marginal ways.

Although the developed world is in a dominant position and has been prepared to use this to further their control of the global economy, the developing countries have not done well in organising themselves to co-ordinate on substantial policy and negotiating positions. The developed countries, on the other hand, are well-organised within their own countries, with well-staffed departments dealing with international trade and finance, and with university academics and private and quasi government think tanks helping to obtain information and map policies and strategies. They also have well-organised associations and lobbies associated with their corporations and financial institutions, which have great influence over the government departments.

On the positive side, globalization has compelled developing countries to improve overall economic management, and make their economies efficient. To get a share of global capital and technology, developing countries have to upgrade their social and economic institutions through administrative, legislative and legal reforms. The quality of governance has to improve to encourage productivity and efficiency. Political stability has to be established. In this context, following lessons can be drawn from East Asian countries:

1. Developing human capital is a basic pre-requisite.

Successful globalization and the knowledge economy require educated, healthy and skilled people.

2. It is necessary to build up domestic savings and put them to productive use.
3. Sound economic management and macro-economic balances are necessary. Large fiscal deficit is a serious obstacle to globalization.
4. Good governance at the national and sub-national levels builds confidence among investors.
5. Transparency has to be established in the functioning of both government and business units.
6. Free and open market economies require effective regulatory authorities because role of government changes from control and regulation to governance and facilitation.
7. Modernised capital markets with effective regulatory authorities are necessary to impart confidence to investors by maintaining stability and regulating speculative forces.

Globalization has helped the smaller, emerging economies gain access to world markets, emergent technologies and collaborations. This has also given them a window to the developed world and helped them understand the significant role of globalization as an instrument, which could be utilised not just to achieve economic efficiency, but also eradicate poverty.

1.2 FDI and Portfolio Investment

Investment in a country by individuals and organisations from other countries is an important aspect of international finance. This flow of international finance may take the form of direct investment (creation of productive facilities) or portfolio investment (acquisition of securities).

FDI is the outcome of the mutual interests of multinational firms and host countries. According to the International Monetary Fund (IMF), FDI is defined as "investment that is made to acquire a lasting interest in an enterprise operating in an economy other than that of the investor. The investor's purpose being to have an effective voice in the management of the enterprise". [1] The essence of FDI is the transmission to the host country of a package of capital, managerial, skill and technical knowledge. FDI is generally a form of long-term international capital movement, made for the purpose of productive activity and accompanied by the intention of managerial control or participation in the management of a foreign firm.

FDI is usually contrasted with portfolio investment which does not seek management control, but is motivated by profit. Portfolio investment occurs when individual investors invest, mostly through stockbrokers, in stocks of foreign companies in foreign land in search of profit opportunities.

However, the distinction between FDI and portfolio investment is not watertight because sometimes FDI policy and portfolio investments are intertwined.

1.3 Superiority of FDI over Other Forms of Capital Inflows

FDI is widely considered an essential element for achieving sustainable development. Even former critics of MNCs expect FDI to provide a stronger stimulus to income growth in host countries than other types of capital inflows. Developing countries are strongly advised to rely primarily on FDI, in order to supplement national savings by capital inflows and promote economic development.

FDI is perceived superior to other types of capital inflows for the following reasons:

1. FDI flows are usually preferred over other forms of external finance because they are non-debt creating, non-volatile and their returns depend on the performance of the projects financed by the investors. FDI also facilitates international trade and transfer of knowledge, skills and technology. In a world of increased competition and rapid technological change, their complimentary and catalytic role can be very valuable.
2. In contrast to foreign lenders and portfolio investors, foreign direct investors typically have a longer-term

perspective when engaging in a host country. Hence, FDI inflows are less volatile and easier to sustain at times of crisis. A recent United Nations report has revealed that FDI flows are less volatile than portfolio flows. To quote, "FDI flows to developing and transition economies in 1998 declined by about 5 percent from the peak in 1997, a modest reduction in relation to the effects on other capital flows of the spread of the Asian financial crisis to global proportions. FDI flows are generally much less volatile than portfolio flows. The decline was modest in all regions, even in the Asian economies most affected by the financial crisis". [2]

3. While debt inflows may finance consumption rather than investment in the host country, FDI is more likely to be used productively.
4. FDI is expected to have relatively strong effects on economic growth, as FDI provides for more than just capital. FDI offers access to internationally available technologies and management know-how, and may render it easier to penetrate world markets.
5. The risk-sharing properties of FDI are undisputed. This suggests that FDI is the appropriate form of external financing for developing countries, which have less capacity than highly developed economies to absorb external shocks. Likewise, the evidence supports the predominant view that FDI is more stable than other types of capital inflows. It is noteworthy that the volatility of FDI remained exceptionally low in the 1990s, when several emerging economies were hit by financial crises.

However, positive growth effects of FDI cannot be taken for granted. The ambiguous, and sometimes contradictory, empirical findings indicate that FDI must no longer be considered to be a homogenous and universally applicable phenomenon in order to improve our understanding of the growth impact of FDI. In the ultimate analysis, it all depends on time-varying and location-specific factors whether FDI and growth are positively correlated or not. For example, opening up early to FDI inflows, combined with close integration into world trade, seems to have strengthened the FDI/growth nexus. The good news for small and less advanced economies is that they can benefit from positive growth effects of FDI as much as large and more advanced developing countries.

1.4 Resource-seeking, Market-seeking and Efficiency-seeking FDI

Three major types of FDI are typically differentiated: resource-seeking FDI, market-seeking FDI and efficiency-seeking FDI.

Resource-seeking FDI is motivated by the availability of natural resources in host countries. This type of FDI was historically important and remains a relevant source of FDI for various developing countries. However, on a world-wide scale, the relative importance of resource-seeking FDI has decreased significantly.

Regarding the history of FDI in developing countries, various empirical studies have shown that the size and growth of host country markets were among the most important FDI determinants. It is debatable, however, whether this is still true with ongoing globalization.

Traditionally, FDI was the only reasonable means to penetrate local markets in various developing countries. For instance, exporting to Latin America was no promising alternative to investing there as local industries were heavily protected. FDI was used to circumvent import barriers. The situation has changed considerably in recent times. Many developing countries have liberalised their import regime, thereby enabling MNCs to choose between exporting or undertaking FDI. As a consequence, purely market-seeking FDI may decline. It is argued that one of the most important traditional FDI determinants, the size of national markets, has decreased in importance, even though conclusive empirical evidence is hard to come by.

The possible decline of market-seeking FDI is largely restricted to FDI in manufacturing industries. Market-seeking FDI received a major push by the opening of service industries to FDI. The bulk of FDI in services, which accounts for a rising share in overall FDI, is market-seeking almost by definition, as most services are not tradable in the sense of cross-border transactions.

Geographically dispersed manufacturing, slicing up the value chain and the combination of markets and resources through FDI and trade are becoming major characteristics of the world economy. Efficiency-seeking FDI, i.e. FDI motivated by creating new sources of competitiveness for firms and strengthening existing ones, may then emerge as the most important type of FDI. Accordingly, the competition for FDI would be based increasingly on cost differences between locations, the quality of infrastructure and business-related services, the ease of doing business and the availability of skills. Obviously, this scenario involves major challenges for developing countries, ranging from human capital formation to the provision of business-related services such as efficient communication and distribution systems.

1.5 Crowding-in and Crowding-out Impacts of FDI

Crowding-in is said to take place when foreign direct investment stimulates new investment in downstream or upstream production by other foreign or domestic producers. While investments in the export sector have the potential for encouraging downstream production, investments in infrastructure encourage upstream production. The MNCs may provide preferential opportunity for exports through access to large internal (inter-firm) markets, which is available only to affiliates set up in host countries. The capital-flow induced growth and the accompanying higher efficiency of the economy may, in turn, induce higher investments.

However, if FDI comes in sectors in which the domestic firms are themselves contemplating investment, the very act of foreign investment may take away the investment opportunities that were open to domestic enterprises. Moreover, if the MNCs raised funds for their expansion programmes from the host country, this might out-compete the domestic firms in the financial markets and thus compete them out. The decision of MNCs for acquisition of domestic firms might similarly lead to large inflow of foreign exchange, appreciating in the process the exchange rate. This might in turn make the host country's export less competitive and thus discourage domestic investment for export markets. All these imperatives may have crowding-out impact on domestic firms.

In view of the double edged nature of FDI, namely the crowding-out and crowding-in effects on domestic industries, the host economies, especially the developing countries have been imposing some kind of *performance requirements* in regard to: (a) local content, (b) export commitment, (c) technology transfer, (d) dividend balancing and (e) foreign exchange neutrality.

These regulations are there to enhance the quality of FDI against the simple increase in the quantity of FDI inflow. Imposition of *performance criteria*, however, comes in the way of the relative openness of the trade regime and may make FDI less attractive for MNCs while deciding the location for their operations. In other words, a trade-off is involved between performance and openness.

1.6 Advantages of FDI for the Host Country

FDI can make up not only for deficiencies in the availability of savings and foreign exchange—which is true of all external flows—but also for weaknesses in domestic entrepreneurial capacity. In other words, the role of FDI in directly stimulating investment activity in the country can be of great significance. This is particularly important for India since there is a likelihood that corporate investment activity may not be dynamic enough to absorb the available resources, particularly in those areas which are being vacated by the public sector. In such a situation, the entrepreneurial function played by FDI can have the effect not only of bringing in additional resources, but also leading to better absorption of domestic savings.

Foreign investment takes place for private gain but it has the following potential benefits for less developed countries (LDCs).

1.6.1 Raising the Level of Investment: Foreign investment can fill the gap between desired investment and locally mobilised savings. Local capital markets are often not well developed. Thus, they cannot meet the capital requirements for large investment projects. Besides, access to the hard currency needed to purchase investment goods not available locally can be difficult. FDI solves both these problems because it is a direct source of external capital. It can fill the gap between desired foreign exchange requirements and those derived from net export earnings.

Foreign investment can stimulate domestic investment through forward and backward linkages. For example, output of a foreign firm can be an input of domestic industries. Similarly, output of the domestic industries can be inputs for the foreign firms. If this is so, foreign firms create demand for industries producing goods purchased by them.

1.6.2 Upgradation of Technology: Production units in developing countries use out-dated equipment and techniques that can reduce the productivity of workers and lead to the production of goods of a lower standard. The ability of domestic producers to compete abroad for export markets is reduced which, in turn, contributes to the difficulties of the developing countries to earn hard currencies. Foreign investment can supply a package of needed resources such as management experience, entrepreneurial abilities, organisational and technological skills. Foreign investment brings with it technological knowledge while transferring machinery and equipment to developing countries.

Similarly, as the foreign-owned enterprise comes into competition with the local firms, the latter category of enterprises are forced to improve their technology and standards of product quality. Further, the foreign-owned enterprises pressurise and assist the local support industries to improve the quality of their products and ensure greater reliability of delivery, both of which make it necessary for the support industries to upgrade their technology.

The indirect effects of FDI on development which arise from the diffusion of technology and other know-how are sometimes more important than the direct effects of FDI. Therefore, one should consider not only the actual transfer of technology but also the spread of better managerial practices and the contribution of FDI to enhancing competition in host country markets. The emphasis on the technology-related spill over effects of FDI is warranted in the light of the fact that most FDI originates from a small number of developed countries which play a dominant role in the development of new technology and that multinational enterprises from these countries dominate the demand and use of new technology. The overall positive effect of FDI in respect of technology is undeniable, whether these effects occur through actual transfers, licensing or through spill over.

With reference to the positive effects of FDI through technology spill over, it has been argued that it varies depending upon the characteristics and policies of host countries, and that the existence of a competitive environment and local technological capabilities is especially important in this regard.

1.6.3 Improvement in Export Competitiveness: FDI can help the host country improve its export performance. By raising the level of efficiency and the standards of product quality, FDI makes a positive impact on the host country's export competitiveness. Further, because of the international linkages of MNCs, FDI provides to the host country better access to foreign markets. Also, where the foreign investment has been made with the specific intention of sourcing parts/components (or even final products) from the host country to take advantage of low cost conditions, FDI contributes to exports directly. Enhanced export possibility contributes to the growth of the host economies by relaxing demand side constraints on growth. This is especially important for those countries which have a small domestic market and must increase exports vigorously to maintain their tempo of economic growth.

1.6.4 Employment Generation: Foreign investment can create employment in the modern sectors of developing countries. Recipients of FDI gain training of employees in the course of operating new enterprises, which contributes to human capital formation in the host country.

1.6.5 Benefits to Consumers: Consumers in developing countries stand to gain from FDI through new products, and improved quality of goods at competitive prices. Moreover, profits generated by FDI contribute to corporate tax revenues in the host country.

1.7 Disadvantages of FDI for the Host Country

FDI is not an unmixed blessing. Governments in developing countries have to be very careful while deciding the magnitude, pattern and conditions of private foreign investment. Possible adverse implications of foreign investment are the following:

1. When foreign investment is competitive with home investment, profits in domestic industries fall, leading to fall in domestic savings.
2. Contribution of foreign firms to public revenue through corporate taxes is comparatively less because of liberal tax concessions, investment allowances, disguised public subsidies and tariff protection provided by the host government.
3. Foreign firms reinforce dualistic socio-economic structure and increase income inequalities. They create a small number of highly paid modern sector executives. They divert resources away from priority sectors to the manufacture of sophisticated products for the consumption

of the local elite. As they are located in urban areas, they create imbalances between rural and urban opportunities, accelerating flow of rural population to urban areas.

4. Foreign firms stimulate inappropriate consumption patterns through excessive advertising and monopolistic/oligopolistic market power. The products made by multinationals for the domestic market are not necessarily low in price and high in quality. Their technology is generally capital-intensive which does not suit the needs of a labour-surplus economy.
5. Foreign firms are able to extract sizeable economic and political concessions from competing governments of developing countries. Consequently, private profits of these companies may exceed social benefits.
6. Continual outflow of profits is too large in many cases, putting pressure on foreign exchange reserves. Foreign investors are very particular about profit repatriation facilities.
7. Foreign firms may influence political decisions in developing countries. In view of their large size and power, national sovereignty and control over economic policies may be jeopardised. In extreme cases, they (foreign firms) may bribe public officials at the highest levels to secure undue favours. Similarly, they may contribute to friendly political parties and subvert the political process of the host country.

Key question, therefore, is how host countries can minimise possible negative effects and maximise positive effects of FDI through appropriate policies.

1.8 World Bank Determinants of FDI

A study of FDI determinants can help policymakers in developing nations to face the challenges arising out of capital inflows. In general terms, their task has various dimensions ranging from human capital formation and capacity-building to the provision of efficient business-related services.

The motivation and determinants of FDI differ among

countries and across economic sectors. These factors include the policy framework, economic determinants and the extent of business facilitation such as macroeconomic fundamentals and availability of infrastructure.

The World Investment Report, 1998 gave a comprehensive list of host country determinants of FDI. The same is reproduced below.

1.8.1 Policy Framework: It includes the following:

1. Economic, political and social stability.
2. Rules regarding entry and operations.
3. Standards of treatment of foreign affiliates.
4. Policies on functioning and structure of markets (especially competition, merger and acquisition policies).
5. International trade and investment agreements.
6. Privatisation policy.
7. Trade policy (tariffs and non-tariff barriers) and coherence of FDI and trade policies.
8. Tax policy.

1.8.2 Economic Determinants: These are as under:

A. Resource/Asset-seeking:

1. Raw materials.
2. Low-cost unskilled labour.
3. Skilled labour.
4. Technological, innovatory and other creative assets (i.e. brand names), including as embodied in individuals, firms and clusters.
5. Physical infrastructure (ports, roads, telecommunications).

B. Market-seeking:

1. Market size and per capita income.
2. Access to regional and global markets.
3. Country-specific consumer preferences.
4. Structure of markets.

C. Efficiency-seeking:

1. Cost of resources and assets, adjusted for productivity of labour resources.
2. Other input costs, e.g. transport and communications costs

to/from and within host economy and costs of other intermediate products.

3. Membership of a regional integration agreement conducive to the establishment of regional corporate networks.

1.8.3 Business Facilitation: It includes the following:

1. Investment promotion (including image-building, investment-generating activities and investment facilitation services).
2. Investment incentives.
3. Hassle costs (corruption, administrative efficiency etc.).
4. Social amenities (bilingual schools, quality of life etc.).
5. Alternate investment services.

When competing for FDI, policymakers have to be aware that various measures intended to induce FDI are necessary and would lead to incremental investment, i.e. investment which will occur only if these measures are taken. In this respect, it becomes imperative to first study the determinants of FDI. These determinants enable policymakers to understand the scale and direction of FDI flows. It enables them in formulating a foreign investment policy that is most conducive to attracting FDI. They are able to concentrate on those factors or areas to which FDI is most sensitive. These normally include liberalisation of FDI regulations and various business facilitation measures.

Another reason to constantly study and review FDI determinants is that those determinants which were sufficient in the past, may prove to be less relevant in the future. The size of local markets appears to be the most important case in point. Similarly, tax incentives which were earlier considered a relatively minor consideration in most FDI decisions are now proven to have become an increasingly important factor in investment decisions. Globalization and the resulting increase in capital mobility have created opportunities for tax competition among countries eager to attract FDI. In the process, tax incentives have assumed new and increasing importance. Globalization can be expected to induce a shift from market-seeking FDI to efficiency-seeking FDI. International competitiveness of local production by foreign investors will then turn out to be a decisive factor shaping the distribution of future FDI. This, in turn, reinforces the role of skilled labour and business facilitation measures.

Endnotes

1. International Monetary Fund, *Balance of Payments Manual*, Washington, DC, 1977, p. 408.
2. United Nations, *World Economic and Social Survey*, 1999, p. 35.

2

Domestic, Regional and International Financial Integration

Financial integration leads to a better diversification of risks and makes a positive contribution to financial stability by improving the capacity of economies to absorb shocks. Financial integration also paves the way for shocks to propagate more quickly among market participants, which could necessitate appropriate safeguards. To mitigate the risks and maximise benefits from financial integration, it is imperative that the financial markets are developed further. Enhanced co-operation among various regulatory authorities is also important for ensuring effective corrective action in an increasingly integrated environment. Further, it is necessary to establish further linkages amongst the various components of financial infrastructure—the trading, payment, clearing, settlement and custodian systems.

2.1 Integration of Financial Markets

2.1.1 Meaning: Integration of financial markets is a process of unifying markets and enabling convergence of risk-adjusted returns on the assets of similar maturity across the markets. The process of integration is facilitated by an unimpeded access of participants in various market segments. Financial markets all over the world have witnessed growing integration within as well as across boundaries, spurred by deregulation, globalization and advances in information technology. Central banks in various parts of the world have made concerted efforts to develop financial markets, especially after the experience of several financial crises in the 1990s.

Expectedly, financial markets tend to be better integrated in developed countries. At the same time, deregulation in developing countries has led to removal of restrictions on pricing of various financial assets, which is one of the pre-requisites for market integration.

Financial market integration encompasses a complex interplay of various factors such as policy initiatives, structure and growth of financial intermediaries, organic linkages among market participants and the preference of savers and investors for financial instruments. The study of integration of financial markets must keep in view the heterogeneity of markets, dimensions of integration, measurement issues and perceived benefits and risks of integration.

Financial market integration at the theoretical level has been postulated in several ways. The most popular economic principles of financial integration include the law of one price, term structure of interest rates, parity conditions such as purchasing power parity, covered and uncovered interest parity conditions, capital asset price model and arbitrage price theory.

2.1.2 Heterogeneous Nature of Financial Markets: Various financial market segments are not uniform as they trade in a variety of instruments which differ in terms of risk and liquidity. Financial markets are heterogeneous due to following reasons:

1. Some market segments are national, whereas others are international in nature, depending on where financial transactions occur among participants within a country's geographic boundary or across the border. Generally, money and credit market segments involving participation of banks and other financial institutions operating within a country's boundary are national in character. Conversely, foreign exchange markets dealing with cross-border transactions and stock markets with cross-listings of securities and participation of foreign institutional investors are international in nature.
2. Financial markets differ in terms of depth and liquidity. For instance, money market instruments are more liquid, while bonds in the capital markets are less liquid.

3. Financial markets differ in terms of economic nature of instruments catering to various needs of economic agents. For instance, a distinction can be made between saving, investment, credit and derivative instruments.
4. Financial markets are differentiated in terms of risk profile of instruments such as government bonds, which do not involve default and credit risks, and corporate bonds, which are relatively more risky in nature. Integration of market segments, thus, reflects an investor's attitude towards risk and the trade-off between risk and return on assets.
5. Market participants in different financial markets could be different such as banks, non-bank financial institutions, including mutual funds, insurance companies, mortgage institutions and specialised long-term financial institutions.

2.1.3 Dimensions of Financial Market Integration: Broadly, financial market integration occurs in three dimensions, nationally, regionally and globally. From an alternative perspective, financial market integration could take place horizontally and vertically. In the horizontal integration, inter-linkages occur among domestic financial market segments, while vertical integration occurs between domestic markets and regional/international financial markets.

A. Domestic Financial Integration: It entails horizontal linkages of various segments, reflecting portfolio diversification by savers, investors and intermediaries. Under horizontal integration, market interest rates typically revolve around a basic reference rate, which is defined as the price of a short-term low-risk financial instrument in a competitive and liquid market. Domestic markets may be closely integrated because intermediaries operate simultaneously in various market segments; for instance, commercial banks operate in both the saving (deposit) and loan markets.

B. Regional Financial Integration: It occurs due to ties between a given region and the major financial centre serving that region. Economic integration might be easier to achieve at a regional level due to network externalities and the tendency of market makers to concentrate in certain geographical centres. Furthermore, regional financial integration can be an important means of developing local financial markets, for instance, through peer pressure to strengthen institutions and upgrade local practices.

C. Global Financial Integration: It refers to the opening up of domestic markets and institutions to the free cross-border flow of capital and financial services by removing barriers such as capital controls and withholding taxes. A deeper dimension of global integration entails removing obstacles to movement of people, technology and market participants across border. Global integration is promoted through harmonisation of national standards and laws, either through the adoption of commonly agreed minimum standards or the mutual recognition of standards.

2.1.4 Measures of Financial Integration: Indicators of financial integration can be classified into *de jure* and *de facto* measures.

The existence of legal restrictions on trade and capital flows across border as well as market segments is the most frequently used *de jure* indicators. However, these indicators have several shortcomings as restrictions may not be binding, or they are not respected. They may not cover a specific aspect of all possible impediments to financial integration.

De facto indicators of financial integration are usually based either on prices or quantities. The commonly used price-based measures for gauging price equalisation and convergence of market segments include cross-market spreads, correlation among various interest rates, tests of common trend in the term structure of interest rates and volatility transmission. Interest rate spreads between the official short-term rate and a benchmark short-term market instrument on the one hand, and various other market interest rates on the other, are used for measuring price convergence and effectiveness of policy.

Price-related measures also include covered and uncovered

interest rate parity as well as asset price correlations between countries. There are, however, serious practical problems in using prices to measure regional or global financial integration, particularly in developing countries. This is because prices may move together because of a common external factor or because of similar macroeconomic fundamentals and not because of market integration. Moreover, prices may be affected by differences in currency, credit and liquidity risks, implying different price movements even if there is a substantial degree of financial integration.

2.1.5 Benefits and Risks of Financial Integration: Though financial integration provides several benefits, it also involves various risks. The benefits and costs of financial market integration depend on the degree of domestic financial market integration, international financial integration and financial development. Evaluating the benefits and risks of financial market integration is a complex issue, particularly in an economy with open capital account.

A. Benefits: The benefits of global integration depend on size, composition, and quality of capital flows. Global financial integration involves direct and indirect or collateral benefits. Analytical arguments supporting financial openness revolve around main considerations such as the benefits of international risk sharing for consumption smoothing, the positive impact of capital flows on domestic investment and growth, enhanced macroeconomic discipline and increased efficiency as well as greater stability of the domestic financial system associated with financial openness. International financial integration could positively affect total factor productivity. Financial openness may increase the depth and breadth of domestic financial markets and lead to an increase in the degree of efficiency of the financial intermediation process by lowering costs and excessive profits associated with monopolistic and cartelised markets, thereby lowering the cost of investment and improving the resource allocation.

B. Risks: Financial market integration also poses some

risks and entails costs. A major risk is that of contagion, which was evident in the case of East Asian crisis and the recent global financial turmoil. Increased domestic and international integration accentuates the risk of contagion as problems in one market segment are likely to be transmitted to other markets with the potential to cause systemic instability.

In the context of globalisation, potential costs include: (a) high degree of concentration of capital flows, (b) misallocation of flows which may hamper their growth effects and exacerbate domestic distortions; (c) loss of macroeconomic stability, (d) pro-cyclical nature of short-term capital flows and the risk of abrupt reversals, (e) a high degree of volatility of capital flows which relates in part to herding and contagion effects, and (f) risks associated with foreign bank penetration.

Direct investment tends to be less volatile than other forms of capital flows. Volatility of capital flows translates into exchange rate instability (under flexible exchange rate) or large fluctuations in official reserves (under a pegged exchange rate regime). Nominal exchange rate volatility may hamper expansion of exports if appropriate hedging techniques are not available to exporters. Large capital inflows can also lead to rapid monetary expansion, inflationary pressures, real exchange rate appreciation and widening of current account deficits.

The nature of optimal integration is highly country-specific and contextual. Financial integration needs to be approached cautiously, preferably within the framework of a plausible roadmap that is drawn up embodying the country-specific context and institutional features. On balance, there appears to be a greater advantage in well-managed and appropriate integration into the global process, which implies not large-scale but more effective interventions by the authorities.

2.2 Domestic Financial Integration

Integration of financial markets assumes importance due to the following reasons:

1. Efficient and integrated financial markets constitute an

important vehicle for promoting domestic savings, investment and consequently economic growth.
2. Financial market integration, by enhancing competition and efficiency of intermediaries in their operations and allocation of resources, contributes to financial stability.
3. Integrated markets serve as a conduit for authorities to transmit important price signals.
4. Integrated financial markets induce market discipline and informational efficiency.
5. Market integration promotes the adoption of modern technology and payment systems to achieve cost effective financial intermediation services.
6. Integrated markets lead to innovations and cost-effective intermediation, thereby improving access to financial services for members of the public, institutions and companies alike.
7. Financial market integration fosters the necessary condition for financial sector of a country to emerge as an international or a regional financial centre.

An important objective of reforms in India has been to integrate the various segments of the financial market for bringing about a transformation in the structure of markets, reducing arbitrage opportunities, achieving higher level of efficiency in market operation of intermediaries and increasing efficacy of monetary policy in the economy. Efficient allocation of funds across the financial sector and uniformity in the pricing of various financial products through greater inter-linkages of financial markets has been the basic emphasis of monetary policy.

In the domestic sphere, integration of markets has been pursued through the following measures:

1. Strengthening competition.
2. Financial deepening with innovative instruments.
3. Easing of restrictions on flows or transactions.
4. Lowering of transaction costs.
5. Enhancing liquidity.

Financial markets in India have also increasingly

integrated with the global financial system as a result of calibrated and gradual capital account liberalisation in keeping with the underlying macroeconomic developments, the state of readiness of the domestic financial system and the dynamics of international financial markets.

Until the early 1990s, India's financial sector was tightly controlled. Interest rates in all market segments were administered. The flow of funds between various market segments was restricted by extensive micro-regulations. There were also restrictions on participants operating in different market segments. Banks remained captive subscribers to government securities under statutory arrangements. The secondary market of government securities was dormant.

In the equity market, new equity issues were governed by several complex regulations and restrictions. The secondary market trading of such equities lacked transparency and depth. The foreign exchange market remained extremely shallow as most transactions were governed by inflexible and low limits under exchange regulation and prior approval requirements. The exchange rate was linked to a basket of currencies. Although the financial sector grew considerably in the regulated environment, it could not achieve the desired level of efficiency. Compartmentalisation of activities of different types of financial intermediaries eliminated the scope for competition among existing financial intermediaries.

Financial markets reform initiated in the early 1990s focused on removal of structural bottlenecks, introduction of new players/instruments, free pricing of financial assets, relaxation of quantitative restrictions, improvement in trading, clearing and settlement practices and greater transparency. Other policy initiatives in the money, the foreign exchange, the government securities and the equity markets were aimed at strengthening institutions, greater transparency, encouraging good market practices, effective payment and settlement mechanism, rationalised tax structures and enabling legislative framework. Dismantling of various price and non-price controls in the financial system has facilitated the integration of financial markets.

Broadly, India's domestic financial market comprises the money market, the credit market, the government securities market, the equity market, the corporate debt market and the foreign exchange market. The channels of integration among various market segments differ. For instance, the Indian money and the foreign exchange markets are intrinsically linked in view of the presence of commercial banks and the short-term nature of both markets. The linkage is established through various channels such as banks borrowing in overseas markets, providing hedging facilities to corporates, accepting foreign currency deposits and acting as conduit for making payments for overseas merchant transactions.

The linkage between the call money and the government securities markets exists, as at times, large positions in government securities are funded through short-term borrowings. The foreign exchange market and the equity markets are linked through the operations of foreign institutional investors. The emerging linkages among the money, the government securities and the foreign exchange markets have at times necessitated the use of short-term monetary measures by the RBI for meeting demand-supply mismatches to curb volatility.

2.3 Regional Financial Integration (Asia)

After the South East Asian crisis of 1997, the geographic scope of cooperation initiatives is expanding across sub-regions of Asia. Asian economies have embarked on various initiatives for regional monetary and financial cooperation.

2.3.1 SEANZA and SEACEN [1]: SEANZA and SEACEN are the oldest initiatives in central bank cooperation in Asia. The SEANZA, formed in 1956, promotes cooperation among central banks by conducting intensive training courses for higher central banking executive positions with the objective to build up knowledge of central banking and foster technical cooperation among central banks in the SEANZA region. The SEACEN provides a forum for member central bank governors to be familiar with each other and to gain deeper understanding of the economic conditions of the individual SEACEN countries. It initiates and facilitates co-operation in research and training relating to the policy and operational aspects of central banking, i.e., monetary policy, banking supervision and payments and settlement systems.

2.3.2 Asian Clearing Union (ACU): ACU—an arrangement of central banking cooperation—is successfully functioning since 1974 for multilateral settlement of payments for promoting trade and monetary cooperation among the member countries. [2] Since 1989, the ACU has also included a currency swap arrangement among its operational objectives.

2.3.3 EMEAP: A more explicit central banking cooperation has been existing in the form of EMEAP since 1991. [3] The ongoing work of EMEAP seeks to further strengthen policy analysis and advice within the region and encourage co-operation with respect to operational and institutional central banking issues. EMEAP central banks have actively coordinated on issues relating to financial markets, banking supervision and payment and settlement systems. The Asian Bond Fund (ABF) initiative of the EMEAP Group has been one of the major initiatives aimed at broadening and deepening the domestic and regional bond markets in Asia. The initiative has been in the form of ABF1 and ABF2. In the near term, the ABF2 Initiative is expected to help raise investor awareness and interest in Asian bonds by providing innovative, low-cost and efficient products in the form of passively managed bond funds. More and more similar kinds of index-driven private bond funds are rapidly emerging in Asia. At present, India does not contribute in the ABF. The informal meeting organised by Asia Cooperation Dialogue (ACD) is, however, attended by participant central banks including India, to discuss promotion of supply of Asian Bonds. The Government of India has given a commitment on participation in the ABF2 to the tune of US$ 1 billion.

2.3.4 SAARCFINANCE: SAARCFINANCE, established in September 1998 is a regional network of the SAARC Central Bank Governors and Finance Secretaries which aims at strengthening the SAARC with specific emphasis on international finance and monetary issues. [4] India has been very actively participating in SAARCFINANCE activities.

2.3.5 ASEAN+3: The countries of ASEAN—Brunei Darussalam, Cambodia, Indonesia, Laos, Malaysia, Myanmar, the Philippines, Singapore, Thailand and Vietnam—and India have entered into a Framework Agreement on comprehensive economic cooperation. The ASEAN has embarked on a process to expand economic cooperation with its neighbours in the north, namely China, Japan and South Korea (ASEAN+3). As far as India's association with ASEAN community is concerned, currently India is not a full-fledged part of the ASEAN network but holds a regular summit with the ASEAN. However, in the years ahead, it is envisaged that ASEAN+3+3 network [5] would help India to share and cooperate on various financial issues as the present network of ASEAN+3 has been consistently engaging in economic policy dialogue of unprecedented scope and depth.

2.3.6 Chiang Mai Initiative: Another instance of central banking cooperation in Asia exists in the form of reciprocal currency or swap arrangements under the Chiang Mai Initiative. [6] The ASEAN Swap Arrangement (ASA) was created primarily to provide liquidity support to countries experiencing balance of payments difficulties. The Finance Ministers of ASEAN+3 announced this initiative in May 2000 with the intention to cooperate in four major areas, *viz.* monitoring capital flows, regional surveillance, swap networks and training personnel.

The clearest evidence of Asian countries' desire to forge closer economic relationships is the proliferation of Free Trade Agreements (FTAs). By 2006, there were more than 30 FTAs under negotiation in East Asia alone. Increasingly, these agreements are also deeper, extending to areas beyond just tariff reduction. An example is the recently signed India-Singapore comprehensive economic cooperation agreement, which covers not only trade in goods, but also services, investments and cooperation in technology, education, air services and human resources.

Regional integration in Asia has improved significantly due to liberalisation measures, formation of several regional cooperation agreements and stronger economic activity in the region. The sharp increase in intra-regional trade indicates that regional economies are better integrated. Regional financial integration is manifested in the price co-movements in the stock, the money and the bond markets. Stock markets in the Asian region are better correlated than the bond and the money markets.

2.4 International Financial Integration

In the wake of globalization, capital has become more mobile across national boundaries as nations are increasingly relying on savings of other nations to supplement the domestic savings. Technological developments in electronic payment and communication systems have substantially reduced the arbitrage opportunities across financial centres, thereby aiding the cross border mobility of funds. Changes in the operating framework of monetary policy, with a shift in emphasis from quantitative controls to price-based instruments such as the short-term policy interest rate, brought about changes in the term structure of interest rates. This has contributed to the integration of various financial market segments. Harmonisation of prudential regulations in line with international best practices, by enabling competitive pricing of products, has also strengthened the market integration process.

Development of financial markets is required for the purpose of not only realising the hidden saving potential and effective monetary policy, but also for expanding the role and participation of a country in the process of globalization, regional and international integration. With growing openness, global factors come to play a greater role in domestic policy formulation, leading to greater financial market integration.

A key feature of global financial integration since early 1980s is the shift in the composition of capital flows to developing and emerging market economies. Private sector flows have outpaced official flows due to increasing liberalisation. Moreover, a shift has occurred in terms of components, from the dominance of debt flows in the 1970s and the 1980s to foreign direct investment (FDI) and portfolio flows since the 1990s. FDI flows have been determined by several push and pull factors, including strong global growth, soft interest rates in home countries, lessening of risks in developing countries, greater business and consumer confidence, rising corporate profitability, large scale corporate restructuring, sharp recovery of asset prices and rising commodity prices.

Trade and FDI openness has encouraged domestic institutional and governance reforms promoting trade and investment further. The hope of better risk sharing, more efficient allocation of capital, more productive investment and ultimately higher standards of living for all have also propelled the drive for stronger regional connections of financial systems across the world. In terms of overall financial flows, Asia has benefited from the surge in net capital flows to emerging markets in recent years.

Greater international financial market integration exposes domestic markets to certain risks and contagion. For instance, global financial imbalances, growing sophistication of financial market participants and the proliferation of complex and highly leveraged financial instruments, including credit derivatives and structured products such as collateralised debt obligations, can heighten volatility in the financial markets. Thus, with growing international integration, there would be a need to be vigilant about the risk profile of financial intermediaries and their vulnerability to abrupt market price shocks. This underlines the need for appropriate risk management strategies as also greater coordination and information sharing among central banks to prevent the transmission of adverse developments abroad to the domestic economy and markets.

With growing financial globalisation, it is important for India to develop financial markets to manage the risks associated with large capital flows. The Report of the Committee on Fuller Capital Account Convertibility, 2006 (Chairman: S.S. Tarapore) observed that in order to make a move towards the fuller capital account convertibility, it needs to be ensured that different market segments are not only well-developed but also that they are well-integrated.

As a result of policy measures undertaken since the early 1990s, India's trade and financial integration has grown with the global economy. The increasing openness of the Indian economy to the external sector in recent years characterises its expanding economic relationships with the rest of Asia. In recent years, the Asian economies are emerging as major trading partners of India.

In tandem with trade openness, India's capital account has witnessed a structural transformation since the early 1990s, with a shift in the composition from official flows to market-oriented private sector flows. From 1950 to 1980, trade balance was financed by capital account balance comprising mainly the official flows. During the 1980s, the dependence on official flows moderated sharply with private debt flows in the form of external commercial borrowing and non-resident Indian (NRI) deposits emerging as the key components of the capital account.

Following the shift in emphasis from debt to non-debt flows in the reform period, foreign investment comprising direct investment and portfolio flows emerged as predominant component of capital account.

To sum up, since early 1990s, there has been a rapid increase in the pace of globalisation, led by growing participation of developing and emerging economies. Financial integration has outpaced trade integration. Cross-border flows of real and financial capital have increased sharply, reflecting the decline in the degree of home bias in capital markets.

The domestic credit market is also getting increasingly integrated with the international capital market as large and creditworthy borrowers have been raising large resources by way of external commercial borrowings. Such corporates are, therefore, less constrained by domestic credit conditions. Raising of resources by banks, the major players in the credit market, by way of external commercial borrowings, *albeit* within limits, has also integrated the domestic and international credit markets. The money market and the government securities market are also integrated as changes in money market rates are quickly transmitted to government securities yields. The linkage between the money market and the credit market also exists even as some stickiness has been observed in the lending interest rate structure. The inter-linkages between the credit market and the bond market are also growing through asset securitisation by banks.

However, the inter-linkages between the equity market on the one hand, and the money, the foreign exchange and the government securities markets on the other, are still weak. The term money market and the private corporate debt market are missing links in the Indian financial markets. There is not much activity in the public issue segment of the corporate debt market, despite availability of good infrastructure, a vibrant equity market and a reasonably developed government securities market. In the corporate debt market, the issuers prefer the private placement segment, which lacks transparency and deprives the retail investor from participating in the debt market.

Regional integration has served as a major catalyst to the global integration process since early 1990s. East and Southeast Asian economies, in particular, have achieved substantial integration. Apart from Asia's growing integration with the rest of the world, increasing integration within Asia also reflects the growing intra-regional trade and financial flows. The stock markets in Asia are more integrated than the money and the bond markets. In the region, Japan, Hong Kong and Singapore serve as the nodal centres for other stock markets. India's trade and financial links with Asia are also growing amidst recent initiatives taken to promote regional cooperation. Emerging Asia has become the *growth centre* of the world due to shifting of production base to the region. This is likely to stimulate greater financial integration in the region.

At the regional level, India's trade links with Asia are growing at a rapid pace, spurred by trade links with China and Southeast Asian countries. Also, India's financial integration with the Asian region has occurred through the linkage of regional stock markets and through modest correlation of bond and money markets.

A key feature of global financial integration since early 1980s has reflected in the shift in the composition of capital flows to developing and emerging market economies, especially from official to private flows. India's financial integration within the region and with the international financial markets is likely to increase in future in view of its robust growth prospects. However, if benefits are to be maximised from a more integrated economy, efforts are needed towards a greater sophistication of financial markets and financial market instruments that allow risks to be shared more broadly and capital to flow into the most productive sectors.

India's integration with the world economy has increased significantly in terms of trade openness and financial integration. Tariff liberalisation and removal of non-tariff barriers have contributed to India's trade integration at global and regional levels. India's capital account has witnessed a structural transformation during the reform period with cross-border non-debt creating private capital flows, emerging as a major component. India is now a major destination for global portfolio equity flows suggesting growing confidence of foreign investors in the Indian economy and financial markets.

Integration among various market segments has grown, especially in the recent period. Growing integration among various financial market segments has been accompanied by lower volatility of interest rates. Financial market integration reflects a dynamic interaction among various parameters such as liquidity, safety and risk, foreign exchange market development, private sector activity, and macroeconomic fundamentals. Alternatively, financial integration exhibits interaction among financial intermediaries, the Government, the private sector and the external sector.

Endnotes

1. The SEANZA refers to South East Asia, New Zealand and Australia. The SEACEN refers to South East Asia Central Banks.
2. At present, its membership includes eight members including India, Islamic Republic of Iran, Nepal, Pakistan and Sri Lanka being the founder members (Myanmar, Bangladesh and Bhutan joined later).
3. Members are the central banks of Australia, China, Hong Kong, Indonesia, Japan, Korea, Malaysia, New Zealand, the Philippines, Singapore and Thailand.
4. SAARCFINANCE members are India, Pakistan, Sri Lanka, Bangladesh, Bhutan, Maldives and Nepal. It is a permanent body, which got formal recognition of SAARC at the 11th SAARC Summit, held in Kathmandu, Nepal in January 2002.
5. India, Australia and New Zealand are included in ASEAN+3+3.
6. Under this Initiative, the total resources available are currently estimated to be around US$ 75 billion (up from less than US$ 40 billion in May 2005), reflecting the renegotiation of most Bilateral Swap Agreements (BSAs).

3

International Investment Position (IIP) of India

A majority of literature on foreign direct investment or on other forms of investment are mainly based on investment flows. Nonetheless, stock of capital, named here as "international investment position (IIP)" is an important instrument to assess a country's financial structure and also its financial stability or instability. If there are any chances of a looming financial crisis in an economy in the near future, one can evince a hint of the upcoming financial crisis in advance by analysing the international investment position in detail. In this chapter, the IIP position of India during the period 2001-2020, has been thoroughly studied by examining the total investments on the assets and liabilities side, components of international investment position and changes in the international investment position during the above period. For the above period, gross foreign assets position, gross foreign liabilities position, net foreign liabilities position and components of IIP were deeply studied. The foreign direct investment (FDI) position is specially focused here.

3.1 What is International Investment Position (IIP)?

IIP, "*is a statistical statement that shows at a point of time, the values and composition of: (a) financial assets of residents of an economy that are claims on non-residents and gold bullion held as reserve assets, and (b) liabilities of residents of an economy to non-residents*" (IMF's Balance of Payments and International Investment Positions Manual 2008, 6th edition, section 7.1).

Most of the advanced economies liberalised much before the 1990s. However, in the post-reforms period, a large number of emerging economies of the world witnessed a huge flow of foreign capital (both inside and outside) which resulted in an enormous increase in the stock of foreign capital. These flows, which are constituents of IIP, are primarily in two types, namely, debt flows and non-debt flows. These are also reflected in the stock of foreign capital, i.e. IIP. Capital flows are characterised by debt creating and non-debt creating capital flows. Non-debt creating flows refer to the flows of financial resources which do not involve any repayment obligations.

Hence, obviously these non-debt creating flows do not create any debt burden on the recipient country. Non-debt creating flows include foreign direct investment (FDI) and foreign portfolio investment (FPI). Among these flows, FDI has a lasting interest for the investing business enterprise. FDI tries to control as well as participate in the management of a business enterprise. FDI is not just a transfer of ownership. FDI usually involves the transfer of factors in addition to capital, including management, technology and organisational skills. Among these two types of private capital flows viz. FDI and FPI, foreign portfolio investment is more volatile in nature. Therefore, FDI can be regarded as a major source of non-debt financial resource for the economic development of a country.

Debt creating capital flows comprise of loans procured from private international commercial banks and financial institutions. Debt flows are assumed to create heavier pressure on a country because of the repayment issues in the form of both interest and principal, while non-debt flows are considered to impose relatively lesser pressure on a country's financial situation because of no repayment obligations. The volume of foreign assets and liabilities, their composition as well as change in the composition over time, are important factors for assessing the health of a country.

IIP is a part of an economy's national balance sheet. Since it is a stock concept, therefore, it is connected to a point of time, generally at the beginning or at the end of a period. It contains all types of foreign capital which are incoming and out flowing.

From the total assets and liabilities listed in an international investment position, one can easily calculate the net foreign assets (NFA) or net international investment position (NIIP) of a country. It is basically the difference between a country's assets and liabilities. It is considered as a country's net foreign wealth position or an indicator of overall financial health, generated from the foreign capital of a country. Similarly, net financial liabilities mean, the difference between a country's liabilities and assets.

A country is called a net external creditor or has net external assets if a country's NIIP is positive i.e. the total foreign assets are greater than the total foreign liabilities. Similarly, if a country is a net external debtor or has net foreign debt, it means that the NIIP is negative, connoting that the total foreign liabilities are higher than the total foreign assets.

Transactions in balance of payment (BOP), price variations of financial assets and liabilities and exchange rate effects are the reasons that changes international investment position.

An IIP has two side entries. First, is the asset side, containing values of foreign assets owned by a country's residents and second, is the liabilities side, containing value of the country's assets owned by foreigners.

Foreign assets have the following components:

1. Foreign direct investment (FDI).
2. Foreign portfolio investment (FPI).
3. Foreign derivatives (FD).
4. Other investments (OI).
5. Foreign reserves.

Foreign liabilities have the following components:

1. Foreign direct investment (FDI).
2. Foreign portfolio investment (FPI).
3. Foreign derivatives (FD).
4. Other investments (OI).

Balance of Payments Manual (BPM) 1993, again

classified foreign portfolio investment as: (a) equity securities, and (b) debt securities, in case of both assets and liabilities.

Other investments are again classified as: (a) monetary authorities, (b) general government, (c) banks, and (d) other sectors, in case of both sides of the IIP.

However, International Financial Statistics Yearbook, 2013, published by IMF, reclassified foreign direct investment (FDI) as: (a) equity and investment fund share, and (b) debt instrument in case of both assets and liabilities. Similarly, foreign portfolio investment (FPI) and other investments were also reclassified. Foreign derivatives have been newly expressed as foreign derivatives (other than reserves) and ESO's (employee stock options).

3.2 Definitions of Various Components

According to the IMF, definitions of the components are as follows.

FDI is defined as "a category of cross-border investment associated with a resident in one economy having control or a significant degree of influence in the management of an enterprise that is resident in another economy".

FPI is defined as cross-border transactions and positions involving debt or equity securities, other than those included in direct investment or reserve assets.

As previously stated, both FDI and FPI plays a very crucial role in international finance. FDI is less volatile and stable than FPI. It is possible that if an economy faces an economic depression, there may be a sudden reversal of FPI. Because of that, an economy can face a severe crisis at that time. In case of FDI, it is safe and comes through multinational corporations with better technology and managerial know-how.

Financial derivatives and employee stock options are financial assets and liabilities that have similar features, such as a strike price and some of the same types of risk elements. A financial derivative contract is a financial instrument that is linked to another specific financial instrument or indicator or commodity and through which specific financial risks (such as interest rate risk, foreign exchange risk, equity and commodity price risks, credit risk, and so on) can be treated in their own right in the financial markets.

Other investments is considered as a residual category which includes positions and transactions other than those included in direct investment, portfolio investment, financial derivatives and employee stock options and reserve assets.

Other investment includes: (i) other equity, (ii) currency and deposits, (iii) loans (including use of IMF credit and loans from the IMF), (iv) non-life insurance technical reserves, life insurance and annuities entitlements, pension entitlements, and provisions for calls under standardised guarantees, (v) trade credits and advances, (vi) other accounts receivable/payable and (vii) SDR allocations (SDR holdings are included in reserve assets).

Reserve assets (RA) are those forms of external assets which are available in the time of need. These are controlled by monetary authorities of an economy. Foreign reserve assets are used for: (i) BOP financing needs, i.e., when there is deficit in balance of payments, (ii) for intervention in exchange markets to affect currency exchange rate, and (iii) for other related purposes like maintaining confidence in the currency and the economy and serving as a basis for foreign borrowing.

3.3 Literature Review

According to Shirai (2009), IIP is an important instrument to judge whether a country is a net external creditor or a net external debtor.

Lane and Milesi-Ferreti (2000) dealt with a theoretical perspective about the importance of gross assets and liabilities, net foreign assets and components of these. The paper also gave an empirical analysis of the determinants for 132 countries, of which 22 were industrial and the remaining were developing countries consisting of sub-Saharan Africa, Middle East and North Africa, Asia, Latin America and transition economies. Data up to 1997 was used for this analysis.

Lane and Milesi-Ferreti (2001) provided an estimate of the stock of foreign assets and liabilities and their equity and debt components for a sample of 67 industrial and developing countries. The data suffered from a number of estimation problems (which they rectified in the 2006 estimate). Nevertheless, the authors provided an extended data series to meet the previous data gap. The data showed that the stock of foreign direct investment and equity in relation to GDP rose for both industrial and developing countries. The paper also addressed the valuation problem occurring from changes in prices and exchange rates.

Fureceri et al. (2011) tried to analyse the medium-term determinants of international investment positions for a large sample of advanced and emerging countries. They emphasized on structural policy as a crucial determinant of international investment position. The analysis involved both cross-sectional and panel data estimation techniques. For a set of 70 countries and time period stretching over 1970-2004 (taking a five year average), the paper used fixed effect regression technique and found that in both the estimations, structural policy settings are important as long-term drivers of gross and net foreign capital positions. Significant determinants included financial development and capital account openness of assets and liabilities, institutional quality regards net foreign assets position and market regulation of foreign assets. More competition-friendly product market regulation, less stringent employment protection legislation, improved institutional quality and greater capital account openness in host countries tended to modify the composition of foreign liabilities towards higher FDI and lesser debt.

In another study, Fureceri, Guichard and Rusticeli (2012) found that the role of structural policies is very important in determining the IIP of a country. According to the paper, "certain kinds of structural policy reforms could help in narrowing global imbalances and modifying the composition of international capital flows towards more stable and productive sources".

Capital account liberalisation is one of the important components in the process of globalization. In a globalised regime, a country experiences rapid capital flows, both inward and outward. This creates challenges for the government policies with respect to the outcome as well as prevention of sudden capital reversals. Composition and size of external assets and liabilities through IIP were used to detect possible risks emanating from such capital reversal (Warsosemito, 2012). Thus, a clear understanding of the IIP and of the relationship between IIP and BOP of a country becomes more and more relevant (Boonstra, 2008).

Scant literature exists on IIP and a part of this is dealing with the relationship between IIP and the balance of payments.

Boonstra (2008) discussed relationship between balance of payments and international investment position of countries. According to Boonstra, "the change in the net international investment position of a country is not only determined by the balance in its current account, but is also strongly influenced by the yield (capital gains or losses) on its holdings abroad minus the yield made by foreign investors in its domestic market".

In a majority of literature, net foreign assets become a central factor. The relationship between current account balance and net foreign wealth of the U.S. economy as well as relationship between savings and current account was analysed by Krugman and Obstfeld (2009).

Prusty et al. (2013) emphasized on the assets-liabilities position of India's investment abroad and tried to examine the trend of assets-liabilities and the net of the two due to India's international investment during the period 2003-10. The paper analysed the components of external assets and liabilities and their growth rates using the RBI data. The paper ends with a suggestion for better policies for building up more assets than liabilities with a view to minimise the negative gap.

Grohe and Uribe (2014) discussed the relationship between current account and NIIP for the U.S. economy and also discussed the valuation change and the NIIP.

US international indebtedness sometimes is measured by net international investment position (Jackson, 2012). This statement is not totally correct, because outflows and inflows of assets have important implications for the value of dollars in international exchange markets.

Another class of literature is on the determinants of the composition of IIP. The composition of the assets and liabilities, the relative success in investing abroad compared to the success of foreign investors in the home market and the currency competition of foreign assets and liabilities are the determining factors (Boonstra, 2008).

Another type of literature on IIP is connected with the possible impact of the existing composition of IIP on the vulnerability of the external sector to any crisis. Warsosemito (2012) studied the Surinam economy and discovered the current stance of the IIP as a tool for detecting possible vulnerabilities in the financial structure. The paper also concluded by analysing the external balance sheet and found that there was no threat to the real economy at all at that stage.

3.4 Why is Inflow of Foreign Assets Needed?

In a closed economy, theoretically, national savings always equals with the national investment. It indicates that a closed economy can increase its wealth only by building up new capital stock. However, for an open economy, the story is something different. An open economy saves either: (i) by building up its capital stock, or (ii) by acquiring foreign wealth through positive trade balance.

Following Krugman and Obstfeld (2009), when an economy is closed, from national income identity we get:

$$Y = C + I + G$$

Where Y: GNP; C: consumption expenditure; I: investment expenditure; and G: government expenditure.

From this identity we get:

$Y - C - G = I$

or, $S = I$ (S stands for national savings).

This implies that national savings is always identically equal with the national investment.

But in case of an open economy, this identity becomes:

$Y = C + I + G + EX - IM$

where EX: export earning; IM: import,

or, $Y - C - G = I + EX - IM$

or, $S = I + CA$ (CA stands for current account balance)

or, $S = I - KA$ (since $CA + KA = 0$ the basic identity).

KA stands for capital and financial account where KA includes capital account, financial account and change in reserve assets.

When $CA < 0$, it signifies that KA must be positive; there would be more capital inflows than outflows. This indicates that liabilities are higher than assets. When $CA > 0$, it signifies that KA must be negative; there would be more capital outflow than inflow. This indicates that assets are higher than the liabilities.

From the above analysis, we can say that when we have surplus in the current account, we invest more abroad, thus making foreign assets higher than the foreign liabilities.

or, $S = I + \Delta NIIP$

[Since, by formula, $NIIP = \sum CA$, or $NIIP_t - NIIP_{t-1} = CA_t$ or $\Delta NIIP = CA$ and since $CA = - KA$, so, $- KA = \Delta NIIP$],

or, When $CA < 0$,

$S = I + KA$

or, $S = I - \Delta NIIP$ (negative $\Delta NIIP$ implies that the change in total liabilities is higher than the change in total assets).

Therefore, inflow of foreign assets can act as a bridge to meet the gap between national savings and investment.

Following Boonstra (2008), the balance of payments statistics are fully compliant with the systems of national accounts. That a current account surplus reflects a national savings surplus follows from the following set of identities:

$Y = C + I + G + (X - M)$ and $Y = C + S + T$,
where,
Y stands for gross national income.
C stands for private consumption expenditure.
G stands for public consumption expenditure.
I stands for gross investment.
S stands for gross savings.
T stands for taxes.
X stands for exports (goods, services, transfers and income from abroad), and
M stands for imports.

Combining these two identities, we get:

$(X - M) = (S - I) + (T - G)$,

where (X – M) states the balance on the current account (CA), (S – I) states the net savings balance of the private sector and (T – G) states the net savings of the public sector.

As a result, (X – M) equals total net national savings, including both private saving and public saving.

For the sake of simplicity here, we do not consider the capital account. This is a relatively smaller balance that includes capital transfers, migrants' transfers and debt forgiveness.

Here, we can treat these transactions as if they are a part of the current account. It is very much important that a direct link between the current account balance and the international investment position of countries comes from the financial account and changes in reserves.

When a country has a surplus in its current account balance, it receives foreign currency, which: (a) either is added to the official reserves (part of the international assets), or (b) is added to the net foreign assets of its banking system.

According to Boonstra (2008), "in the real world, its residents will acquire foreign assets (such as direct investments or portfolio investments), which are recorded as a gross outflow in its financial account. At the same time, foreign investors will acquire assets in a country (adding to its liabilities), which will be recorded as a gross inflow in the financial account.

Net acquisition of foreign assets (measured as a net outflow in the financial account) plus the changes in net reserves, is a direct link between the balance of payments and international investment position.

As the overall balance of payments by definition equals zero, we can work from the identity that CA + NFA + RES + EO = 0 (which equals CA = – FA – RES –EO), reflecting the balance respectively in the current (CA) and financial (FA) accounts and the changes in reserves (RES). EO denotes errors and omissions, thereby reflecting the statistical inaccuracies. It may be noted that a negative sign in FA and RES reflect a net increase in foreign assets.

3.5 Variables and Analysis

Here, we will understand the components of international investment position and net international investment position (liabilities position) in respect of the GDP. Also, we will check components of international investment position in percentage terms against total assets and liabilities. Investment data was collected from the International Financial Statistics Yearbook published by the IMF from online database. GDP data was taken from the World Bank's online databank (last year's GDP data [2020] was taken from statistia.com). All the data is in millions of US dollars.

We have defined our variables as:

NFA = Assets – Liabilities...(1)

NFDIA = FDI Assets – FDI Liabilities...(2)

NFPIA = FPI Assets – FPI Liabilities...(3)

NFDA = Financial Derivatives Assets – Financial Derivatives Liabilities...(4)

NOIA = Other Investment Assets – Other Investment Liabilities...(5)

Negative of any of the five items would be considered as net liabilities.

RASSET = Reserve Assets.

Theoretically, (1) = (2) + (3) + (4) + (5)...(6)

Our purpose here is to study the pattern of NIIP and patterns of different components of assets and liabilities of IIP, mainly the FDI.

Here, we have also considered another concept, which is related to the intensity of crisis or can be taken as an indicator of financial crisis (Shirai, 2009) in an economy. This is denoted as

$NFL_{it} = [(FL_{it} - FA_{it})*100]/GDP_{it}$

NFL_{it} is net foreign liabilities. This measure indicates the net position of a country in respect of foreign investment. NFL indicates investments received by a country less investment made by that country in the rest of the world. It is measured as a percentage of the GDP.

Strength of a country's external sector depends on the foreign reserves a country holds. So, we have also presented foreign reserves minus gold as a percentage of the GDP. A country can come out of an emergent crisis if it has a substantial amount of foreign reserves. Foreign reserves are defined as:

$RA_{it} = [(RA - G)_{it}*100]/GDP_{it}$

Where, RA stands for reserve assets less gold. This RA is also presented as a percentage of the GDP.

High populated countries like India need foreign capital for its economic development. During the last few decades, India has been the centre of attraction for foreign investors because of its high growth potential and also because our economy is in a transitional stage. Primarily, during the post-globalization period, India has experienced enormous capital flows.

India has achieved an improvement in IIP during the study period aforementioned. For India, gross foreign liabilities for the entire period had been always higher than the gross foreign assets. This indicates that the inflows of foreign capital for the entire period were higher than the outflows and India is considered as a net external debtor or in other words, has net foreign debt.

Figure 3.1 presents the trend of gross foreign assets and liabilities as percent of GDP.

Figure 3.1: Gross Foreign Assets and Gross Foreign Liabilities as Percent of GDP

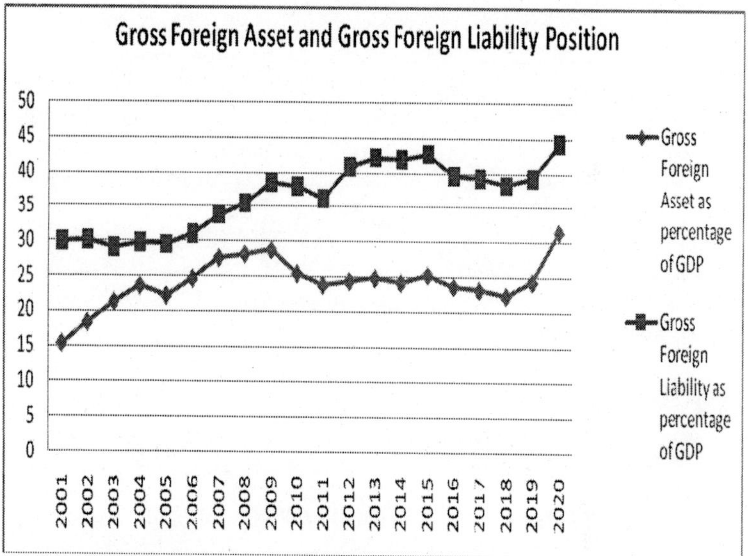

Source: International Financial Statistics Yearbook, IMF and World Bank's online data, www.worldbank.org.

It is quite discernible from the above figure that the liabilities have been continuously increasing. However, post the financial crisis, gross foreign assets reduced as a percent of GDP. Nonetheless, in recent years, gross foreign assets have been witnessing an upsurge. This means that the Indian economy is getting more and more integrated with the rest of the world.

Figure 3.2 presents the trend of FDI assets and liabilities as a percent of GDP. It is quite clear that over the period, liabilities position (FDIL) shows a rising trend but from 2009 onwards, assets position (FDIA) has not changed significantly. FDIL as a percentage of GDP was much higher than FDIA as percentage of GDP. This means that FDI inflow in India was much higher than the FDI outflow.

Figure 3.2: FDI Assets and FDI Liabilities as Percent of GDP

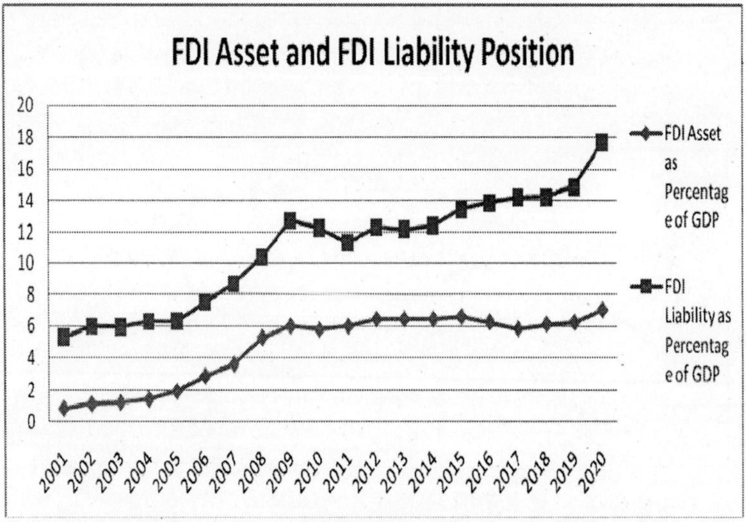

Source: International Financial Statistics Yearbook, IMF and World Bank's online data, www.worldbank.org.

Fianancial derivatives, one of the components of international investment position, has been absent in the case of India. Table 3.1 shows net foreign liabilities positions (NFL) and its compoments such as NFDIL, NFPIL, NOIL, RASSET. From equation (6) it can be written that, NFL = NFDIL + NFPIL + NOIL − RASSET. Asout;ined in Table 3.1, NFDIL (i.e. net FDI inflows as percentage of GDP) rose from 4.47 percent in 2001 to 10.67 percent in 2020. NFDIL were smaller than NFPIL, NOIL and RASSET initially but imrpoved gradually and consequently, NFDIL was higher than NFPIL in 2020. RASSET has also holds a significant position. Table 3.1 has also been diagramatically presented as Figure

3.3., which will be helpful to comprehend with the statistics at a glance.

Table 3.1: Net Foreign Liabilities Positions (NFL) and its Components

(Percentage of GDP)

Year	NFL	NFDIL	NFPIL	NOIL	RASSET
2001	14.60	4.47	6.44	15.10	11.41
2002	11.81	4.88	6.07	15.47	14.62
2003	7.78	4.77	6.79	13.91	17.70
2004	6.25	4.88	7.82	13.58	20.03
2005	7.33	4.40	7.61	13.64	18.31
2006	6.46	4.66	7.77	12.87	18.85
2007	6.23	5.07	10.02	13.77	22.62
2008	7.39	5.16	7.60	15.97	21.34
2009	9.83	6.74	8.65	15.57	21.13
2010	12.62	6.49	9.86	14.05	17.77
2011	12.43	5.31	8.76	14.70	16.34
2012	16.48	5.85	10.09	16.84	16.29
2013	17.41	5.75	9.61	18.00	15.95
2014	17.73	5.96	10.48	17.10	15.82
2015	17.51	6.83	10.63	16.70	16.64
2016	16.01	7.59	9.54	14.54	15.67
2017	16.08	8.37	9.97	13.19	15.45
2018	15.99	8.09	8.96	13.53	14.60
2019	15.00	8.62	9.13	13.31	16.06
2020	12.83	10.67	9.92	13.88	21.64

Source: International Financial Statistics Yearbook, IMF and World Bank's online data, www.worldbank.org.

Figure 3.3 presents all the components of IIP. It is clear from the Figure that all of the net liabilities components in India portray its position as a net borrower except for the reserve assets. The significant finding is that the net liabilities were least for the most stable type of flow, i.e., FDI and much lower for more volatile flows like FPI and other debt-creating flows.

Evidently, during course of time, the trend of NFDIL has

been increasing and in the most recent year viz. 2020, NFDIL was slightly higher than NFPIL.

Figure 3.3: Comparison between NFDIL, NFPIL, NOIL and RASSET

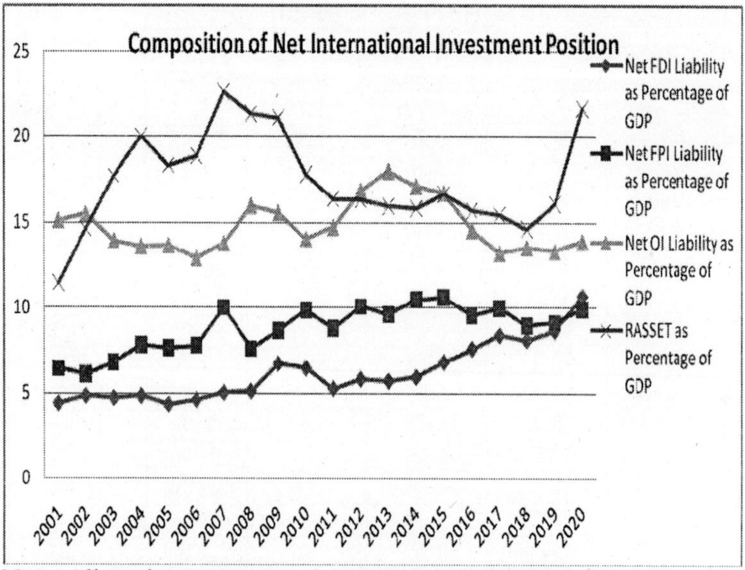

Note: All entries are expressed as percentage of GDP.
Source: International Financial Statistics Yearbook, IMF and World Bank's online data, www.worldbank.org.

From the Figure, it is clear that the flows which were unstable (FPI) and the flows (OI) which were a burden for the economy because of repayment of principal and interest, were a major part of total foreign liabilities.

This may cause severe problems for the country in future in the sense that in the face of a crisis, a significant part of the GDP might be used to pay back the FPIs.

Net foreign liabilities (NFL) position [measured as foreign liabilities minus foreign assets] and expressed as a percentage of GDP, rose between 2003 and 2014 and thereafter started falling till 2020 (Figure 3.4).

A fall in NFL is assumed to be a good sign for the economy.

Figure 3.4: Net Foreign Liabilities Position as Percentage of GDP

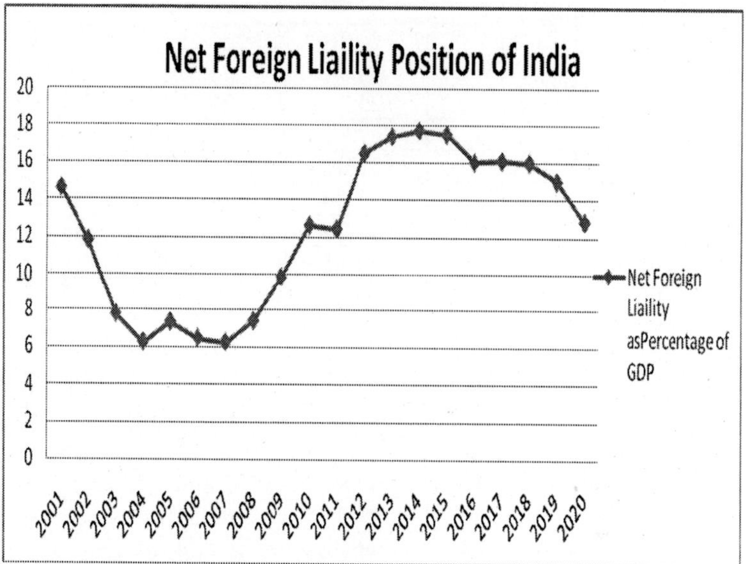

Source: International Financial Statistics Yearbook, IMF and World Bank's online data, www.worldbank.org.

Table 3.2 depicts that FDI liabilities increased in proportion of total liabilities from 17.70 percent in 2001 to 40.03 percent in 2020 and FDI assets in proportion of total assets increased from 5.44 percent in 2001to 22.44 percent in 2020. This basically means that Indians are making inward FDI in higher proportions.

Table 3.2 further shows that FPI in total liabilities was more than 20 percent throughout, which is a cause for concern keeping in mind the volatility of FPI flows.

Table 3.2: Proportion of FDIA in TA and Proportion of FDIL, FPIL and OIL in TL (in percent)

Year	FDIA/TA	FDIL/TL	FPIL/TL	OIL/TL
2001	5.44	17.70	21.97	60.33
2002	6.10	19.89	20.62	59.48
2003	5.71	20.58	23.54	55.88
2004	6.01	21.09	26.40	52.51
2005	8.63	21.36	26.22	52.42
2006	11.67	24.24	25.37	50.38
2007	13.13	25.70	29.78	44.51
2008	18.77	29.38	21.50	49.12
2009	20.95	33.07	22.61	44.32
2010	22.74	32.24	26.18	41.58
2011	25.20	31.22	24.36	44.42
2012	26.49	30.12	24.88	45.00
2013	26.02	28.91	22.93	48.17
2014	26.68	29.62	25.18	45.20
2015	26.17	31.41	25.03	43.56
2016	26.53	34.96	24.28	40.75
2017	25.26	36.24	25.69	38.07
2018	27.49	37.14	23.65	39.21
2019	25.75	37.84	23.64	38.53
2020	22.44	40.03	22.84	37.13

Source: International Financial Statistics Yearbook, IMF.

Figures 3.5 (a) and Figure 3.5 (b) portray a comparative study of different components of liabilities between 2001 and 2020. As is evident in the Figures, in 2001, among the total liabilities, 18 percent consisted of FDI, 22 percent of FPI and 60 percent of OI.

Also, we can deduce from the Figures, that in 2020, among the total liabilities, FDI increased to 40 percent, FPI increased to 23 percent and other investments reduced to 37 percent. The comparative study also shows that FDI increased much more than the FPI, and OI reduced, during the 20 years study period.

Figure 3.5 (a): Components of Liabilities in 2001

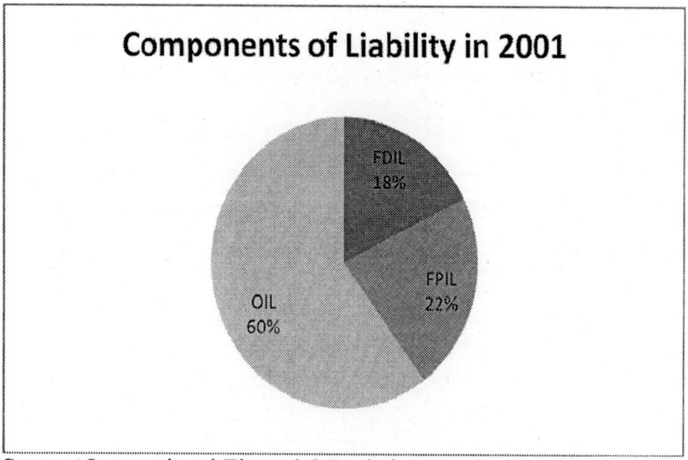

Source: International Financial Statistics Yearbook, IMF.

Figure 3.5 (b): Components of Liabilities in 2020

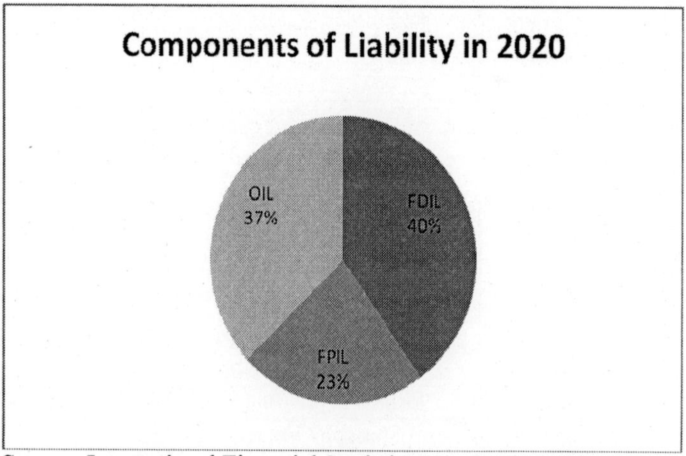

Source: International Financial Statistics Yearbook, IMF.

Moving further, we now discuss the composition of assets and liabilities in FDI. Table 3.3 presents statistics about the assets and liabilities in FDI, comprising of equity and investment fund share (IFS) and debt instrument. For assets, equity and IFS as percentage of FDI, they reduced from 95.14 percent in 2001 to 64.20 percent in 2020. Debt instruments as percentage of FDI increased from 4.86 percent in 2001 to 35.80 percent in 2020.

Table 3.3: Share of Equity and Investment Fund Share (IFS) and Debt Instruments as Assets and Liabilities in FDI (percent)

Year	Assets		Liabilities	
	Equity and IFS /FDI	Debt/FDI	Equity and IFS /FDI	Debt/FDI
2001	95.14	4.86	93.44	6.56
2002	94.87	5.13	93.09	6.91
2003	92.80	7.20	93.51	6.49
2004	90.56	9.44	92.67	7.33
2005	87.69	12.31	93.69	6.31
2006	89.18	10.82	94.99	5.01
2007	88.36	11.64	96.01	3.99
2008	85.51	14.49	95.94	4.06
2009	80.80	19.20	96.00	4.00
2010	77.03	22.97	96.88	3.12
2011	73.65	26.35	95.80	4.20
2012	71.21	28.79	95.56	4.44
2013	69.04	30.96	95.18	4.82
2014	69.30	30.70	95.58	4.42
2015	68.41	31.59	95.34	4.66
2016	67.02	32.98	95.67	4.33
2017	66.05	33.95	95.81	4.19
2018	65.95	34.05	95.69	4.31
2019	65.19	34.81	94.72	5.28
2020	64.20	35.80	94.66	5.34

Source: International Financial Statistics Yearbook, IMF.

Interestingly, in case of liabilities, there was no significant change at all. Hence, there was a growing trend for investment in debt securities in the case of assets while in the case of liabilities, equity and IFS was higher than 92 percent. This particular trend is surely a positive sign for a country's external sector.

The present study reveals that from both assets and liabilities side of IIP, FDI as percentage of GDP raised steadily, except for few years during the period 2001-2020. Due to the high growth potential and as a transition economy, India attracted FDI and huge FDI liabilities were witnessed in this period. During the period of financial crisis (2008-09), India was less affected from both the assets and liabilities side. Comparing with 2001, the proportion of FDI assets in total assets and the proportion of FDI liabilities in total liabilities, increased in 2020. Perhaps, lesser risk, better technology and managerial know-how made FDI an important component of the IIP. However, the pattern of components of net foreign liabilities position, as percentage of GDP, shows that FPI liabilities as well as other liabilities, including debt liabilities, were higher than the FDI liabilities for the entire period except for 2020.

It is pertinent to note here that a continuously rising FDI component in total liabilities is a good indicator of India's external health. The policy always should be such that it aims at controlling the flows which are of volatile nature and try to encourage stable and non-debt creating flows like FDI.

4

International Financial Integration (IFI) of India

This chapter outlines and discusses the concept and different dimensions of IFI with focus on India's international financial integration.

An economy needs capital to improve its overall condition by building up economic and social infrastructure. By this, a country can enhance production, create more employment opportunities, and reduce poverty. Foreign capital is very important for the economic growth as well as for the economic development of a country, especially in the case of an underdeveloped economy, which does not have sound capital base and requires greater capital for its development.

There are a number of ways to build up a sound capital base of a country. One of the ways is by increasing the domestic savings and transforming those savings into investment. It is, however seen, that a domestic economy is often unable to provide sufficient investments for its own development. Sometimes, a domestic economy also lacks in updated technology for improving its own production structure. In such cases, foreign capital becomes one of the important sources of capital requirement of a country and in the process the country receives improved technology too.

4.1 Types of International Flows of Capital

International capital flows is of two types viz. inflow and outflow. As a generalized perception, it is found that developed countries invest more in outflows than what they receive in foreign capital and underdeveloped countries receive more in foreign capital than what they invest outward. The opposite phenomenon is more obvious, which is known as the *allocation puzzle* (Gourinchas and Jeanne, 2007).

Since 1990s, restrictions on cross-border capital flows have been reduced—especially in the developing economies—by opting for different policies and removal of barriers, which has led to an enormous rise in cross-border capital flows for a majority of countries of the world. This has definitely added to the stock of foreign capital.

Some valuation adjustments resulting from changes in the valuation of flow balances brought forward from prior periods also have to be done apart from considering the effects of inadvertent accounting errors and omissions (Offermanns and Pramor, 2007). With a rise in both inward and outward flows of foreign capital, foreign liabilities and foreign assets of a country become more integrated with the rest of the world. Accordingly, international financial integration assumes significance with opening up of the economies.

4.2 Financial Integration

Ho (2009) defined financial integration as 'the process through which financial markets in an economy become closely integrated with those of other economies in the rest of the world'. Financial integration is a process which can take place in a number of ways like: (i) sharing of information and technologies by firms and financial institutions located in different countries, (ii) sharing of best practices by different financial institutions regards transactions in newly engineered financial products among the economies, and (iii) using cross-border capital flows,

In this book, cross-border capital flows are used to define international financial integration. Although a lot of research has already been carried out with regards to global capital flows, studies on stock of foreign investment are limited. Such studies are important for different reasons. Analyzing the stock of foreign investment of a country can lend an idea about the financial structure of an economy. Not only that, the net foreign liability position of a country is an indicator of the net creditworthiness of a country and gives signal about the possibility of financial crisis and the quantum of foreign exchange reserves, thereby revealing the strength of an economy.

The concept of international financial integration is based on the external/foreign assets and liabilities a country holds. Its absolute measure shows how much a country is integrated with the capital market of the world and the other measures depicting the composition, give an indication of the degree of instability it may possibly have.

A detailed study on the trends and composition of international financial integration of a country can provide an understanding of the strength of its external sector. Since the trends as well as the composition of international financial integration of a country depends on several factors—both domestic and external—a study on the determinants of international financial integration would extend a representation regarding which factors should be taken care of if a country has to keep a strong and stable external capital account so that they may withstand any shock, more often an external one, which has the possibility of generating fluctuations in the balance of payments and consequently an economic crisis.

As already mentioned, although a lot of studies on trends, composition and determinants of foreign capital flows are available, yet only a few are at disposal regards international financial integration. Additionally, most of the literature is focused on the developed countries. However, it is important to note, that the emerging economies are experiencing higher capital flows since they opened up for external capital flows and are thus getting more and more integrated with the rest of the world. Amongst these countries, some are still having income much lower than the advanced economies.

IIP consists of a two-sided entry, namely, assets comprising of value of foreign assets owned by a country's residents and the other being the liability comprising of the value of the country's assets owned by foreigners. Foreign assets encompass: (a) foreign direct investment (FDI), (b) foreign portfolio investment (FPI), (c) foreign derivatives (FD), (d) other investments (OI) and (e) foreign reserves. Foreign liabilities include: (a) foreign direct investment (FDI), (b) foreign portfolio investment (FPI), (c) foreign derivatives (FD) and (d) other investments (OI). Balance of Payments Manual (BPM) 1993, further classified foreign portfolio investment as equity securities and debt securities for both assets and liabilities.

4.3 Literature Review

Lane and Milesi-Ferreti (2003) discussed broad trends of volume-based and equity-based measures of international financial integration from 1983 to 2001 for 14 high income countries. They found that for both these measures, an increasing trend was witnessed in international financial integration and also in dispersion of volume-based measure of international financial integration, especially from 1992.

Agenor (2001) provided a detailed theoretical analysis regarding the costs and benefits of international financial integration. The paper opined that for a small and open developing economy, the benefits of international financial integration are long-term in nature whereas the costs of international financial integration exist only in short period. The risks should not be high so as to hinder the long-run benefits and reversal of policy decisions. Therefore, proper management and preparation is necessary to achieve long-term benefits.

Reserve Bank of India (2007) stated that the benefits of global integration depend on the size, composition and quality of capital flows. According to the paper, "the benefits and costs of financial market integration depend on the degree of domestic financial market integration, international financial markets integration and financial development. Evaluating the benefits and risks of financial market integration is a complex issue, in particular, in an economy with an open capital account".

Levine (2001) opined that international financial integration could positively affect total factor productivity. Through financial openness, the depth and breadth of domestic financial markets may increase and can lead to an increase in the degree of efficiency of the financial intermediation process by lowering costs and excessive profits associated with the monopolistic and cartelized markets, thereby lowering the cost of investment and improving resource allocation (Levine, 1996; Caprio and Honhan, 1999).

Empirical studies on international financial integration have shown mixed results pertaining to the benefits of financial integration. With increased globalization, possible costs may include a high degree of concentration of capital flows and misallocation of flows, which may hamper the growth effects and exacerbate domestic distortions, ultimately leading to loss of macroeconomic stability. The pro-cyclical nature of short-run capital flows and the risk of its abrupt reversals make total foreign capital flows highly unstable and raise risks associated with foreign bank penetration (Dadush, Dasgupta and Ratha; 2000).

It is interesting to state that most studies find that compared to other forms of capital flows, direct investment tends are less volatile (Chuhan *et al.*, 1996; Brewer and Nollen, 2000; Sarno and Taylor, 1999). A judgemental view is required on whether and when a country has reached the 'threshold'. The nature of optimal integration is highly country-specific and contextual.

Financial integration needs to be handled cautiously, preferably within the framework of a plausible roadmap that is drawn up embodying the country specific context and institutional features. There appears to be a greater advantage in proper management and appropriate integration with the global process, implying not large-scale but more effective interventions by the authorities.

Vo and Daly (2007) showcased trends of international financial integration (stock of assets and liabilities as percent of GDP) for a set of 79 countries for the period 1980-2003 and concluded that there was a rising trend, meaning thereby that stock of liabilities only as share of GDP was also rising.

Lane and Milesi-Ferretti (2008) stated that the speed of cross-border financial integration was especially rapid for the high-income countries, since the main driving force was the impact of financial innovation on international asset trade among countries with highly-developed financial systems. A second driving force was the creation of Euro, as the elimination of currency risk and the associated deepening of the Euro-denominated financial markets generated a discrete increase in cross-border asset trade among member countries. These forces were very important in credit markets.

Lane (2010) portrayed trends in international financial integration for Euro area countries for the period 1999-2007. The paper highlighted currency composition of foreign assets and foreign liabilities as an important dimension of international balance sheet to understand the sources and implications of shifts in net positions over the last decade. It was found that European Union member countries had dramatically expanded cross-border financial positions since the creation of Euro, as it eliminated currency risk and the deepening of the area created wide markets thereby generating a discrete increase in cross-border financial trade.

Arfaoui and Abaoub (2010) mainly focused on the determinants of international financial integration. They studied 15 international stock markets and observed that international financial integration, measured as summation of assets and liabilities as percent share of GDP, rose during the period 1988-2008.

Acharya and Prakash (2013) concluded that removal of entry barriers promotes competition at the international level and reduces cost of funds and financial services. To finance investment, a liberalized market and availability of different financial sources, reduces not only the funding costs but also the fund availability risk for a borrower. For international investors, availability of various risk instruments improves risk return profile. It brings in, new financial techniques and products. It also forces financial intermediaries to go for innovation and be competitive. However, the authors argued that a high degree of financial integration involves some costs. A high level of IFI, caused by excessive capital inflows, lead to an appreciation of local currency, resulting in loss of competition in international goods market. Alongside, too much outflow of capital, triggers panic in financial markets and makes the operation of economic policies hostage to it.

International financial integration has been one of the most important areas of international finance in recent times. General perception is that globalization results in greater financial integration through cross-border asset trade. All the countries did not globalize simultaneously. Whereas, most of the advanced economies or high income countries globalized much earlier, middle income and low income countries globalized much later.

Hence, it is assumed that quantum and pattern of cross-border flows for the three sets of countries may not be the same. There may be differences in level and composition of international financial integration of different countries on the basis of differences in income, differences in the history of capital flows and host of other factors. Before we go on to examine what determines the level and composition of IFI, it is necessary to inspect the trends and composition of international financial integration of different countries.

4.4 Different Measures of IFI

International financial integration is measured by total assets and liabilities and also by its components. Based on observations made by Lane and Milesi-Ferretti (2003), the following parameters of international financial integration are noticeable:

1. $IFIVB_{it} = [(FA_{it} + FL_{it})*100]/GDP_{it}$
2. $IFIEQ_{it} = [(PEQA_{it} + FDIA_{it} + PEQL_{it} + FDIL_{it})*100]/GDP_{it}$

3. $IFIDEBT_{it} = [(DA_{it} + DL_{it})*100]/GDP_{it}$
4. $IFIFDI_{it} = [(FDIA_{it} + FDIL_{it})*100]/GDP_{it}$

Where, FA and FL refer to the stocks of aggregate foreign assets and liabilities. PEQA stands for portfolio equity asset, PEQL is portfolio equity liability, FDIA is denoted as foreign direct investment asset and FDIL is foreign direct investment liability. DA and DL are debt asset and debt liability respectively.

Measure 1 indicates how much a country's financial capital market is integrated with the world's capital market through foreign investment assets and liabilities. This is a volume-based measure of international financial integration (IFIVB) (Lane and Milesi-Ferretti, 2003) and is measured as percentage of GDP. This measure is an overall measure of international financial integration and other measures are its components.

Measure 2 is the equity-based measure of international financial integration (IFIEQ) (Lane and Milesi-Ferretti, 2003). Equity-based measure of international financial integration takes equity components of foreign investment assets and liabilities. Equity components comprise of both foreign direct investment equity and foreign portfolio equity. Since segregated measure of FDI into equity and debt is not available, we have taken total FDI as equity. Also, in general, FDI debt is very small in comparison to FDI equity. Therefore, considering total FDI in place of FDI equity does not harm our analysis to any significant extent. The equity-based measure of international financial integration is also taken as a percentage of GDP.

Measure 3 reflects debt-based measure of international financial integration (IFIDEBT). This indicates how much a country invests in other countries of the world in the form of debt and how much debt a country takes from other countries. This measure is taken as a percentage of GDP. Measure 4 is the FDI measure of international financial integration. IFIFDI measures a country's integration in terms of inward and outward FDI investments.

4.5 Descriptions of the Components of IFI

FDI can be defined as "a category of cross-border investment associated with a resident in one economy having control or a significant degree of influence in the management of an enterprise that is resident in another economy". FPI is defined as a cross-border transaction and position involving debt or equity securities, other than those included in direct investment or reserve assets.

Both FDI and FPI, play an important role. FPI is more volatile and unstable than FDI. During economic downswings, there is a possibility of sudden reversal of FPI and consequently, an economy can face a severe crisis. It is generally accepted that FDI is safe and comes with better technology and managerial know-how through multinational corporations.

Financial derivatives and employee stock options are financial assets and liabilities that have common features, such as a strike price and similar types of risk elements. A financial derivative contract is a financial instrument that is linked to another specific financial instrument or indicator or commodity and through which specific financial risks (such as interest rate risk, foreign exchange risk, equity and commodity price risks, credit risk, and so on) can be treated.

Other investment is a residual category that includes positions and transactions other than those included in direct investment, portfolio investment, financial derivatives and employee stock options and reserve assets. Other investment consists of: (a) other equity, (b) currency and deposits, (c) loans (including use of IMF credit and loans), (d) non-life insurance technical reserves, life insurance and annuities entitlements, pension entitlements, and provisions for calls under standardised guarantees, (e) trade credits and advances, (f) other accounts receivable/payable, and (g) SDR allocations (SDR holdings are included in reserve assets).

The categories "debt assets" and "debt liabilities" include sum of "portfolio debt securities" and "other investment" (but not FDI inter-company debt, which is in the FDI statistics). Reserve assets are those external assets that are readily available to and controlled by monetary authorities for meeting balance of payments financing needs, for intervention in currency exchange markets, and for other related purposes (such as maintaining confidence in the currency and the economy, and serving as a basis for foreign borrowing).

4.6 International Financial Integration of India

The below paragraphs discuss international financial integration in India. As is discernible from Table 4.1 that since volume based measure is the total of foreign assets and liabilities, this measure is of the highest value.

Table 4.1: Volume Based, Equity and Debt Based Measures of IFI in India (percent)

Year	IFIVB	IFIEQ	IFIDEBT
2001	45.32	10.09	21.05
2002	48.53	11.06	20.42
2003	50.40	12.55	18.60
2004	53.48	13.86	17.78
2005	51.82	14.93	17.36
2006	55.73	16.92	18.46
2007	61.43	20.72	16.35
2008	63.69	21.53	18.94
2009	67.34	25.81	18.63
2010	63.49	26.15	17.60
2011	60.09	23.42	17.52
2012	65.25	25.90	19.94
2013	67.01	25.84	22.66
2014	66.08	26.02	20.78
2015	68.03	26.85	20.56
2016	63.34	26.37	17.80
2017	62.40	26.01	16.69
2018	60.66	25.51	16.52
2019	63.66	26.42	17.00
2020	75.77	31.15	19.02

Source: International Financial Statistics Yearbook, IMF and World Bank's online data, www.worldbank.org.

From Figure 4.1, a rising trend could be witnessed, going up from 45 percent in 2001 to 76 percent in 2020. Equity measure of IFI was in the third position up to 2006 and it was lower than the debt measure of IFI. 2007 onwards and till 2020, equity measure of IFI was higher than the debt measure. Pertinently, it is a good sign for the economy that proportion of debt components in aggregate has been falling, though at a very slow rate.

Figure 4.1: Trend of Different Measures of IFI of India

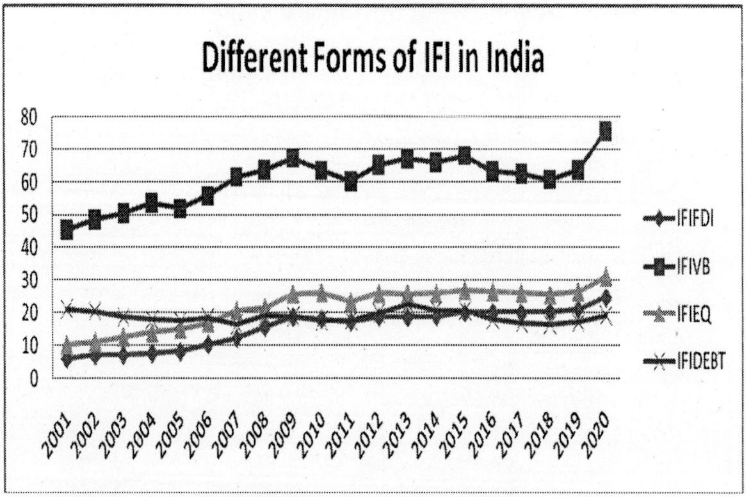

Table 4.2 shows FDI integration of India for the period 2001-2020. As is evident from the table, FDI integration rose continuously, starting from 6 percent in 2001 to 25 percent in 2020. Except between 2009 and 2011, there was a fall in IFIFDI. This may be due to the negative impact of international financial crisis of 2007-08. It is a very positive dimension for the Indian economy that it is investing more and more (both inward and outward) in stable and low risk forms of investment.

This is evident from Figure 4.2.

Table 4.2: FDI-based Measure of IFI in India (percent)

Year	IFIFDI
2001	6.14
2002	7.12
2003	7.20
2004	7.72
2005	8.24
2006	10.41
2007	12.32
2008	15.73
2009	18.78
2010	18.05
2011	17.33
2012	18.77
2013	18.66
2014	18.86
2015	20.04
2016	20.15
2017	20.07
2018	20.37
2019	21.15
2020	24.79

Source: International Financial Statistics Yearbook, IMF and World Bank's online data, www.worldbank.org.

Table 4.3 presents summary of different measures of IFI. As mentioned previously, IFIVB is the highest among the four because of its composition of total assets and total liabilities. Standard deviation is also the highest in IFIVB.

In this chapter, we have introduced the concept of international financial integration. Here, we have used four measures of IFI. It is revealed that the trend of IFIVB is rising, going up from 45 percent in 2001 to 76 percent in 2020. Equity measure of IFI was in the third position up to 2006 and was lower than the debt measure of IFI. 2007 onwards and till 2020, equity measure of IFI was higher than the debt measure.

Figure 4.2: Trend of FDI Integration of India

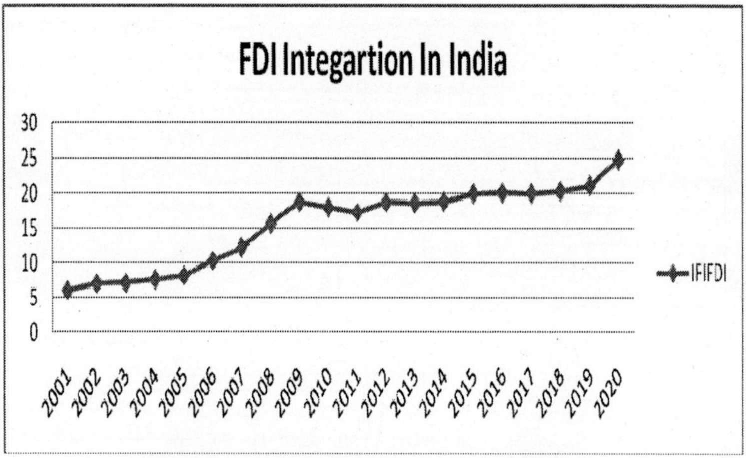

Table 4.3: Summary Statistics of Different Measures of IFI of India

	IFIFDI	IFIVB	IFIEQ	IFIDEBT
Mean	15.59500	60.67600	21.85550	18.68400
Median	18.35500	62.87000	25.66000	18.53000
Maximum	24.79000	75.77000	31.15000	22.66000
Minimum	6.140000	45.32000	10.09000	16.35000
Std. Dev.	5.774232	7.598663	6.276423	1.731639
Skewness	-0.456845	-0.362528	-0.671781	0.592902
Kurtosis	1.795198	2.624572	2.072292	2.511157
Jarque-Bera	1.905315	0.555543	2.221500	1.370916
Probability	0.385715	0.757470	0.329312	0.503859
Sum	311.9000	1213.520	437.1100	373.6800
Sum Sq. Dev.	633.4933	1097.054	748.4763	56.97288
Observations	20	20	20	20

Source: International Financial Statistics Yearbook, IMF and World Bank's online data, www.worldbank.org.

It is a good sign for the economy that proportion of debt components in aggregate has been falling, albeit at a slow rate.

Debt measure of IFI for the entire period was around 19 percent. It can witnessed, that FDI integration has been continuously rising from 6 percent in 2001 to 25 percent in 2020. Except from 2009 to 2011, there was a fall in IFIFDI.

5

Financial Leveraging of India

In recent years, especially in the post-globalized period, growing flow of trade and capital has become a central phenomenon of economic interaction. In recent times, plethora of literature is available, dealing with various aspects of global capital flows. These studies focus on the causes, consequences, and policy responses to recent surges in international capital flows. Some of the studies have pointed out several puzzling aspects also.

International investment position has come up as an important area of current research, primarily focussed on studying the net outcome of global capital flows [Offermanns and Pramor, 2007; Lane and Milesi-Ferretti 2001, 2006]. As international payments and investment positions claim a growing share of both corporate and national balance sheets, they also inevitably impact domestic financial variables and the level and composition of economic activity.

The studies have attempted to estimate the investment position of countries. It is generally found that the means of individual NFA/GDP (net financial asset to gross domestic product) ratios show large differences between the country groups.

The studies have found that industrial countries have exhibited an almost entirely negative position in recent times; whereas both the rise and the subsequent fall experienced by emerging markets are much more pronounced. Developing countries still started from a similar negative position, but displayed a substantial deterioration throughout the 1980s with further subsequent decline and no major trend reversal.

As was rightly pointed out by International Monetary Fund in its World Economic Outlook (2014), increase in the foreign holdings of domestic liabilities raised the possibilities of different types of financial crises, including banking, currency, sovereign debt and sudden stops.

A closer investigation of the evidence that has been presented below suggests that it is foreign-held debt that poses a risk. Levchenko and Mauro (2007) studied the behaviour of several types of flows, and found that portfolio debt and bank flows had a major role in propagating the crisis during periods of sudden stops, while FDI was stable and portfolio equity played a limited role. Furceri et al. (2012), found that large debt inflows increased the probability of banking, currency and balance-of-payment crises, while FDI or portfolio equity inflows had a negligible effect.

The peculiarity that industrial countries exhibit almost an entirely negative position as a consequence of global capital flow in the recent times, calls for further probe.

5.1 Indications of Financial Leveraging of India

Since liability is associated with repayment of money, therefore, it is much more important than the asset side of a balance sheet. Total debt of a country is the summation of FPI debt, FDI debt, financial derivatives and other investments. Total equity is the summation of FDI and FPI equity. It should be noted here that proportion of FDI debt is very small in comparison with FDI equity.

Financial leverage can be measured by debt to debt plus equity ratio. If the ratio is increasing then it can be said that financial leverage exists. Sometimes, only debt to equity ratio is used to calculate financial leverage.

Financial leverage can be defined as:

1. Debt equity ratio: [(FDI Debt + FPI Debt + Other Debt)/ (FDI Equity + FPI Equity)].
2. Debt to debt plus equity ratio: [(FDI Debt + FPI Debt + Other Debt)/(FDI Equity + FPI Equity + FDI Debt + FPI Debt + Other Debt)].

Financial leverage of India is presented in Table 5.1 while

deliberating on the debt to equity component. In absolute volumes, both have shown a rising trend. After 2010, equity was higher than the debt. From 2016 onwards, debt to equity ratio was very close to 1 in case of India (Table 5.1).

Table 5.1: Measures of Financial Leverage of India during 2001-2020

Year	Debt to Debt Plus Equity	Debt to Equity
2001	0.70	2.39
2002	0.69	2.19
2003	0.62	1.66
2004	0.60	1.50
2005	0.58	1.36
2006	0.56	1.29
2007	0.51	1.03
2008	0.56	1.25
2009	0.50	1.01
2010	0.48	0.91
2011	0.53	1.15
2012	0.54	1.17
2013	0.56	1.25
2014	0.55	1.21
2015	0.54	1.19
2016	0.51	1.05
2017	0.50	1.01
2018	0.51	1.05
2019	0.51	1.04
2020	0.48	0.92

Source: International Financial Statistics Yearbook, IMF.

Figure 5.1 shows the total debt liability and total equity liability of India during the period 2001-2020.

While scanning the two measures of financial leverage, debt to equity ratio was observed as falling for India from the liability side. In 2020, it was less than 1, meaning thereby that equity was higher than the debt (Figure 5.2), which is a healthy sign.

Figure 5.1: Total Debt Liability and Total Equity Liability of India during 2001-2020

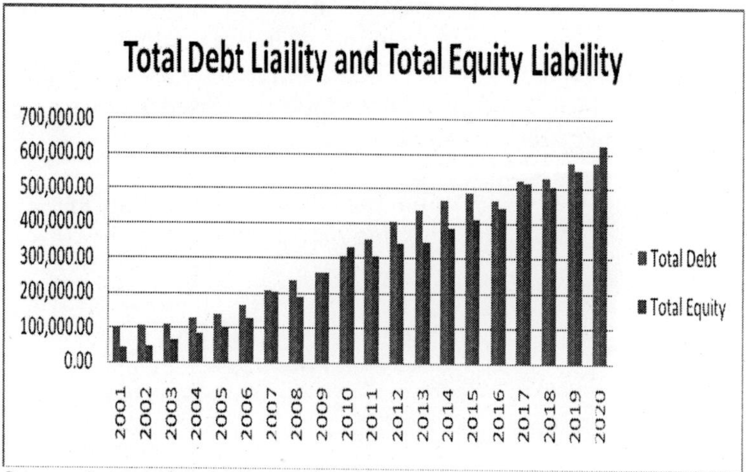

Source: International Financial Statistics Yearbook, IMF.

Figure 5.2: Total Debt to Equity Liability of India during 2001-2020

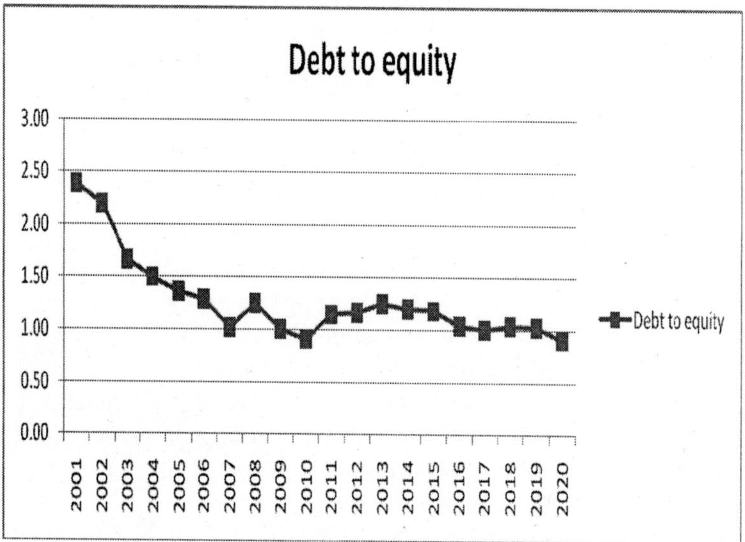

Source: International Financial Statistics Yearbook, IMF.

Figure 5.3 depicts the second measure. Bhattacharya et al. (2015) observed that for the developed countries, there was an indication of financial leverage in the twenty-first century. However, for developing countries, there was no indication of financial leverage up to 2012. Data of recent years also points out that debt to debt plus equity ratio witnessed a downward trend and in 2020, it came below the 0.5 level.

Figure 5.3: Total Debt to Debt Plus Equity Liability of India during 2001-2020

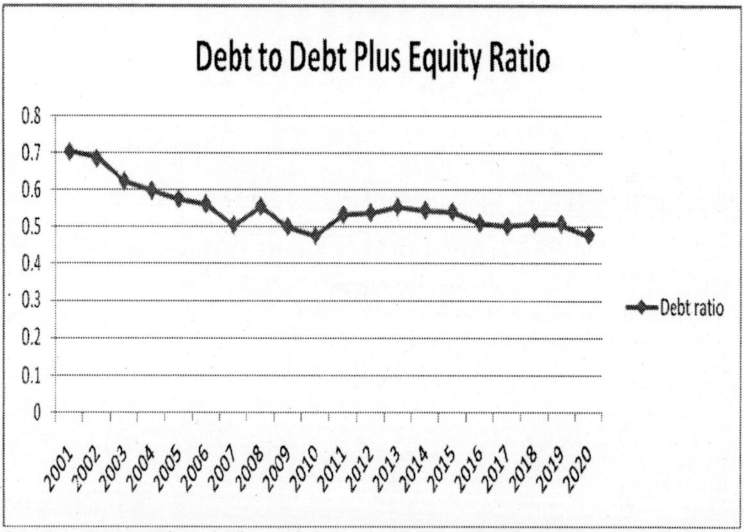

Source: International Financial Statistics Yearbook, IMF.

Generally, it can be said that both FDI and FPI have been growing in India. All the developed countries in this study possessed a positive net foreign direct investment, i.e., they invested in the rest of the world for increased participation in the management control of domestic companies and institutions, while not encouraging much FDI participation in their companies and institutions. However, they do raise finance from the rest of the world through debt securities except Japan (Bhattacharya et al., 2015). For all the five developing countries considered, average net FDI was negative whereas for the developed countries, it was the opposite case.

FDI is expected to come with Greenfield investment, better technology and know-how and thus may exert a positive effect on the real economy of the recipient country. Contrarily, FPI is more volatile and risky especially portfolio debt and can create net debt liability, leading to financial crises. Therefore, countries should be aware of their negative net debt positions and pursue policies accordingly.

6

General Conditions, Legislations, Rules and Regulations Governing FDI

Foreign direct investment (FDI) is considered as a major source of non-debt financial resource for the economic development. FDI flows into India have grown consistently since liberalization and are an important component of foreign capital since FDI infuses long term sustainable capital in the economy and contributes towards technology transfer, development of strategic sectors, greater innovation, competition and employment creation amongst other benefits. Therefore, it is the policy of the Government of India to attract and promote FDI in order to supplement domestic capital, technology and skills for accelerated economic growth and development. FDI, as distinguished from foreign portfolio investment, has the connotation of establishing a *lasting interest* in an enterprise that is resident in an economy other than that of the investor.

6.1 Economic Reforms and FDI

Foreign investment policy in the post-reforms period has emphasised greater encouragement and mobilisation of non-debt creating private inflows for reducing reliance on debt flows. Progressively liberal policies have led to increasing inflows of foreign investment in the country.

The initial policy stimulus to FDI in India came in July 1991 when the new industrial policy provided, *inter alia*, automatic approval for projects with foreign equity participation up to 51 percent in high priority areas. In recent years, the Government has initiated the second generation reforms under which measures have been taken to further facilitate and broaden the base of FDI in India. The policy for FDI allows freedom of location, choice of technology, repatriation of capital and dividends. As a result of these measures, there has been a strong surge of international interest in the Indian economy. The rate at which foreign direct investment inflow has grown during the post-liberalisation period is a clear indication that India is fast emerging as an attractive destination for overseas investors.

As part of the economic reforms programme, policy and procedures governing foreign investment and technology transfer have been significantly simplified and streamlined. Presently, foreign investment is freely allowed in all sectors including the services sector except in cases where there are sectoral ceilings.

It is the intent and objective of the Government of India to attract and promote foreign direct investment (FDI) in order to supplement domestic capital, technology and skills, for accelerated economic growth. FDI, as distinguished from portfolio investment, has the connotation of establishing a *lasting interest* in an enterprise that is resident in an economy other than that of the investor.

India has one of the most transparent and liberal FDI regimes among the emerging and developing economies. By FDI regime is meant those restrictions that apply to foreign nationals and entities but not to Indian nationals and Indian owned entities. The differential treatment is limited to a few entry rules, spelling out the proportion of equity that the foreign entrant can hold in an Indian (registered) company or business. There are a few banned sectors (like lotteries and gaming and legal services) and some sectors with limits on foreign equity proportion. The entry rules are clear and well-defined and equity limits for foreign investment in selected sectors such as telecom quite explicit and well- known.

6.2 Regulatory Framework

The Government has put in place a policy framework on

foreign direct investment (FDI), which is transparent, predictable and easily comprehensible. This framework is embodied in the Circular on Consolidated FDI Policy, which is updated from time-to-time to capture and keep pace with the regulatory changes, effected in the interregnum. Department for Promotion of Industry and Internal Trade (DPIIT), Ministry of Commerce and Industry, Government of India makes policy pronouncements on FDI through press notes/press releases which are notified by the Department of Economic Affairs (DEA), Ministry of Finance, Government of India as amendments to the Foreign Exchange Management (Non-Debt Instruments) Rules, 2019 under the Foreign Exchange Management Act, 1999 (42 of 1999) (FEMA).

These notifications take effect from the date of issue of Press Notes/Press Releases,, unless specified otherwise therein. The payment of inward remittance and reporting requirements are stipulated under the Foreign Exchange Management (Mode of Payment and Reporting of Non-Debt Instruments) Regulations, 2019 issued by the Reserve Bank of India (RBI). The regulatory framework, over a period of time, thus, consists of FEMA and Rules/Regulations thereunder, Consolidated FDI Policy Circular, press notes, press releases, clarifications, etc.

The Consolidated FDI Policy Circular subsumes and supersedes all previous press notes, press releases, clarifications and circulars issued by DPIIT. The information given in this book is based on the Consolidated FDI Policy Circular which became effective from October 15, 2020.

6.3 Entities Eligible to Invest in India

These include the following:

1. A non-resident entity can invest in India, subject to the FDI Policy except in those sectors/activities which are prohibited. However, a citizen of Bangladesh or an entity incorporated in Bangladesh can invest only under the Government route. Further, a citizen of Pakistan or an entity incorporated in Pakistan can invest, only under the

Government route, in sectors/activities other than defence, space and atomic energy and sectors/activities prohibited for foreign investment.

2. NRIs resident in Nepal and Bhutan as well as citizens of Nepal and Bhutan are permitted to invest in the capital of Indian companies on repatriation basis, subject to the condition that the amount of consideration for such investment shall be paid only by way of inward remittance in free foreign exchange through normal banking channels.
3. A company, trust and partnership firm incorporated outside India and owned and controlled by NRIs can invest in India with the special dispensation as available to NRIs under the FDI Policy.
4. Foreign institutional investors (FIIs) and Foreign portfolio investors (FPIs) may in terms of Schedule 2 and 2A of FEMA (Transfer or Issue of Security by Persons Resident Outside India) Regulations, as the case may be, respectively, invest in the capital of an Indian company under the Portfolio Investment Scheme.
5. Only registered FIIs/FPIs and NRIs as per Schedules 2,2A and 3 respectively of Foreign Exchange Management (Transfer or Issue of Security by a Person Resident Outside India) Regulations, 2000, can invest/trade through a registered broker in the capital of Indian Companies on recognised Indian Stock Exchanges.
6. A SEBI registered Foreign Venture Capital Investor (FVCI) may contribute up to 100 percent of the capital of an Indian company engaged in any activity mentioned in Schedule 6 of Notification No. FEMA 20/2000, including start-ups irrespective of the sector in which it is engaged, under the automatic route.
7. A non-resident Indian may subscribe to National Pension System governed and administered by Pension Fund Regulatory and Development Authority (PFRDA), provided such subscriptions are made through normal banking channels and the person is eligible to invest as per

the provisions of the PFRDA Act. The annuity/accumulated saving will be repatriable.

6.4 Entities into Which FDI Can Be Made (i.e. Eligible Investee Entities)

FDI can be made into the following entities:

1. **FDI in an Indian Company:** Indian companies can issue capital against FDI.
2. **FDI in Partnership Firm/Proprietary Concern:** A non-resident Indian (NRI) or a person of Indian origin (PIO) resident outside India can invest in the capital of a firm or a proprietary concern in India on non-repatriation basis subject to specified conditions.
3. **FDI in Trusts**: FDI is not permitted in trusts other than in VCF registered and regulated by SEBI and Investment Vehicle.
4. **FDI in Limited Liability Partnerships (LLPs)**: FDI in LLPs is permitted subject to specified conditions.
5. **Investment Vehicle:** An entity being *investment vehicle* registered and regulated under relevant regulations is permitted to receive foreign investment from a person resident outside India.
6. **Start-up Companies:** Start-ups can issue equity or equity-linked instruments or debt instruments to FVCI against receipt of foreign remittances, as per the FEMA regulations. In addition, start-ups can issue convertible notes to person resident outside India subject to specified conditions.
7. **FDI in other Entities**: FDI in resident entities other than those mentioned above is not permitted.

6.5 Entry Routes for Investment

Investments can be made by non-residents in the equity shares/fully, compulsorily and mandatorily convertible debentures/fully, compulsorily and mandatorily convertible preference shares of an Indian company, through the automatic route or the government route. Under the automatic route, the non-resident investor or the Indian company does not require any approval from Government of India for the investment.

Under the government route, prior approval of the Government of India is required. Proposals for foreign investment under government route are considered by respective Ministries/Departments of the Government.

6.6 Caps on Investments

Investments can be made by non-residents in the capital of a resident entity only to the extent of the percentage of the total capital as specified in the FDI policy. The caps in various sector(s) are detailed in chapter 7 of this book.

6.7 Important Rules and Regulations Governing Foreign Investments in India

6.7.1 Repatriation of Capital: Foreign capital invested in India is generally allowed to be repatriated along with capital appreciation, if any, after the payment of taxes due on them, provided the investment was approved on a repatriation basis.

6.7.2 Repatriation of Dividends and Profits: Profits and dividends earned in India are repatriable after the payment of taxes due on them. No permission of RBI is necessary for effecting remittance, subject to compliance with certain specified conditions.

6.7.3 Acquisition of Immovable Property by a Non-resident: A person resident outside India, who has been permitted by RBI to establish a branch, or office, or place of business in India (excluding a liaison office), has general permission of RBI to acquire immovable property in India that is necessary for, or incidental to, the activity. However, in such cases a declaration in prescribed form is required to be filed with RBI within 90 days of the acquisition of immovable property. Foreign nationals of non-Indian origin who have acquired immovable property in India with the specific approval of RBI cannot transfer such property without prior permission from the RBI.

6.7.4 Acquisition of Immovable Property by Non-resident Indian (NRI): An Indian citizen resident outside India can acquire by way of purchase any immovable property in India other than agricultural/plantation/farm house. He may transfer any immovable property other than agricultural or plantation property or farm house to a person resident outside India who is a citizen of India or to a person of Indian origin resident outside India or a person resident in India.

6.8 Post-approval Procedures

6.8.1 Project Clearances: After the approval has been obtained, the applicant may get his unit/company registered with the Registrar of Company. Subsequently, the company needs to obtain various clearances such as land clearance, building design clearance, pre-construction clearance, labour clearance etc. from different authorities before beginning its operations. These clearances differ from sector to sector and may also differ from state to state.

6.8.2 Registration and Inspection: Each industrial unit is supposed to maintain records in regard to production, sale and export, use of specified raw materials including public utilities like water and electricity, labour related details, financial details and details in regard to industrial safety and environment.

The unit is also subject to periodic inspection by the factory inspector, labour inspector, food inspector, fire inspector, central excise inspector, air and water inspector, mines inspector, city inspector and the like, the list of which may go up to thirty or more.

6.8.3 Foreign Exchange Management Act (FEMA), 1999: The additional provisions which apply only to entry of FDI emanate from the provisions of FEMA. According to FEMA, no person resident outside India, shall without the approval/knowledge of the RBI, may establish in India a branch or a liaison office or a project office or any other place of business.

6.9 Entry Options for Foreign Investors

A foreign company planning to set up business operations in India has the following options:

Incorporate a company under the Companies Act, 1956 through:

- Joint venture or;
- Wholly-owned subsidiary.

Foreign equity in such Indian companies can be up to 100 percent depending on the requirements of the investor, subject to equity caps in respect of the sector/area of activities under the FDI policy.

Enter as a foreign company through:

- Liaison office/representative office.
- Project office.
- Branch office.

Such offices can undertake activities permitted under the Foreign Exchange Management Regulations, 1999.

6.9.1 Incorporation of a Company: For registration and incorporation, an application has to be filed with the Registrar of Companies. Once a company has been registered and incorporated as an Indian company, it is subject to Indian laws and regulations as applicable to other domestic Indian companies.

6.9.2 Liaison Office/Representative Office: The role of the liaison office is limited to collecting information about possible market opportunities and providing information about the company and its products to prospective Indian customers. It can promote export/import from/to India and also facilitate technical/financial collaboration between the parent company and companies in India. A liaison office cannot, however, undertake any commercial activity, directly or indirectly, and cannot, therefore, earn any income in India. Approval for the establishment of a liaison office in India is given by the Reserve Bank of India (RBI).

6.9.3 Project Office: Foreign companies planning to execute specific projects in India can set up temporary project/site offices in India. The RBI has now granted general permission to foreign entities to establish project offices subject to specified conditions. Such offices cannot undertake or carry on any activity other than relating and incidental to the execution of the projects. Project offices may remit the surplus of the project on completion outside India, a general permission for which has been granted by the RBI.

6.9.4 Branch Office: Foreign companies engaged in manufacturing and trading activities abroad are allowed to set up branch offices in India for the following purposes:

1. Export/import of goods.
2. Rendering professional or consultancy services.
3. Carrying out research work in which the parent company is engaged.
4. Promoting technical or financial collaboration between Indian companies and parent or overseas group company.
5. Representing the parent company in India and acting as buying/selling agent in India.
6. Rendering services in information technology and development of software in India.
7. Rendering technical support to the products supplied by the parent/group companies.
8. Foreign airline/shipping company.

A branch office is not allowed to carry out manufacturing activities on its own but is permitted to sub-contract these to an Indian manufacturer. Branch offices established with the approval of the RBI may remit outside India the profit of the branch net of applicable Indian taxes and subject to RBI guidelines. Permission for setting up branch offices is given by the RBI.

6.9.5 Branch Office on *Stand-Alone Basis* in Special Economic Zones (SEZs): Such branch offices would be isolated and restricted to the SEZ and no business activity/transaction will be allowed outside the SEZ in India, which include branches/subsidiaries of their parent office in India.

No approval shall be necessary from the RBI for a company to establish a branch/unit in SEZs to undertake manufacturing and service activities, subject to specified conditions.

6.9.6 Investment in a Firm or a Proprietary Concern by NRIs: A non-resident Indian (NRI) or a person of Indian origin (PIO) resident outside India may invest by way of contribution to the capital of a firm or a proprietary concern in India on non-repatriation basis provided:

1. The amount is invested by inward remittance or out of specified account types (NRE/FCNR/NRO accounts) maintained with an Authorised Dealer.
2. The firm or proprietary concern is not engaged in any agricultural/plantation or real estate business, i.e. dealing in land and immovable property with a view to earning profit or earning income therefrom.
3. The amount invested shall not be eligible for repatriation outside India. NRIs/PIOs may invest in sole proprietorship concerns/partnership firms with repatriation benefits with the approval of Government/RBI.

6.9.7 Investment in a Firm or a Proprietary Concern by Other Than NRIs: No person resident outside India other than NRI/PIO shall make any investment by way of contribution to the capital of a firm or a proprietorship concern or any association of persons in India. The RBI may, on an application made to it, permit a person resident outside India to make such an investment subject to such terms and conditions as may be considered necessary.

To sum up, subject to certain foreign equity conditions, a foreign company can set up a registered company in India and operate under the same laws, rules and regulations as applicable to an Indian-owned company. Unlike many countries including China, India extends National Treatment to foreign investors. There is no discrimination against foreign companies registered in India or in favour of domestically owned ones. There is, however, a minor restriction on those foreign entities which entered a particular sub-sector through a joint venture with an Indian partner. If they want to set up another company in the same sector, they must get a no-objection certificate from the joint venture partner. This condition is explicit and transparent unlike many hidden conditions imposed by some other recipients of FDI. There are also a few prudential conditions on the sale of shares in unlisted companies and the above market price sale of shares in public companies.

The new policies have substantially relaxed restrictions on foreign investment, industrial licensing and foreign exchange. Capital market has been opened to foreign investment and banking sector controls have been eased. As a result of the various policy initiatives taken, India has been rapidly changing from a restrictive regime to a liberal one and FDI is encouraged in almost all economic activities under the automatic route. The Government is committed to promoting increased flow of FDI for better technology, modernisation, exports and for providing products and services of international standards. Therefore, the policy of the government has been aimed at encouraging foreign investment, particularly in core infrastructure sectors so as to supplement national efforts.

7

Sector-specific Caps and Conditions on FDI for Permitted Sectors

7.1 Prohibited Sectors

FDI is prohibited in the following sectors:

1. Lottery business including Government/private lottery, online lotteries etc.
2. Gambling and betting including casinos etc.
3. Chit funds.
4. Nidhi company.
5. Trading in Transferable Development Rights (TDRs).
6. Real estate business or construction of farm houses. Real estate business shall not include development of townships, construction of residential and/or commercial premises, roads or bridges and Real Estate Investment Trusts (REITs) registered and regulated under the SEBI (REITs) Regulations 2014.
7. Manufacturing of cigars, cheroots, cigarillos and cigarettes, of tobacco or of tobacco substitutes.
8. Activities/sectors not open to private sector investment, e.g. atomic energy and railway operations (other than permitted activities).

Foreign technology collaboration in any form including licensing for franchise, trademark, brand name, management contract is also prohibited for lottery business and gambling and betting activities.

7.2 Permitted Sectors

Investments can be made by non-residents in the capital of a resident entity only to the extent of the percentage of the total capital as specified in the FDI policy. Investments by non-residents can be permitted in the capital of a resident entity in certain sectors/activity with entry conditions. Such conditions may include norms for minimum capitalization, lock-in period etc. Besides the entry conditions on foreign investment, the investment/investors are required to comply with all relevant sectoral laws, regulations, rules, security conditions, and state/ local laws/regulations.

In the sectors/activities mentioned in Tables 7.1 to 7.6, FDI up to the limits indicated against each sector/activity is allowed, subject to applicable laws/regulations, security and other conditions. In sectors/activities not listed in Tables 7.1 to 7.6, FDI is permitted up to 100 percent under the automatic route, subject to applicable laws/regulations; security and other conditions.

Wherever there is a requirement of minimum capitalization, it shall include share premium received along with the face value of the share, only when it is received by the company upon issue of the shares to the non-resident investor. Amount paid by the transferee during post-issue transfer of shares beyond the issue price of the share, cannot be taken into account while calculating minimum capitalization requirement.

Sectoral cap, i.e. the maximum amount which can be invested by foreign investors in an entity, unless provided otherwise, is composite and includes all types of foreign investments, direct and indirect.

Foreign investment in sectors under government approval route resulting in transfer of ownership and/or control of Indian entities from resident Indian citizens to non-resident entities will be subject to government approval. Foreign investment in sectors under automatic route but with conditions, resulting in transfer of ownership and/or control of Indian entities from resident Indian citizens to non-resident entities, will be subject to compliance of such conditions.

Any existing foreign investment already made in accordance with the policy in existence would not require any modification to conform to amendments introduced. The onus of compliance of above provisions will be on the investee company.

7.3 FDI in Agriculture and Allied Sectors

Agricultural sector occupies a key position in the Indian economy. Agriculture (inclusive of animal husbandry, forestry and fishing) is central to the nutrition needs of India and also remains the largest sector of India's economy as a source of employment.

Agricultural products like cereals (mainly rice), tea, coffee, cashew, spices, tobacco and leather are important items of India's exports and hence foreign exchange earnings. Agriculture is also the source of raw material for agro-based industries including textiles, cigarettes, jute, sugar, paper, processed foodstuffs and *vanaspati.*

Moreover, agricultural sector provides market for capital goods (tractors, pump sets and other agricultural machinery), inputs (fertilisers, insecticides), and light consumer goods. The nation has invested huge resources for the development of agriculture under various plans.

The development of the agricultural sector depends, to a large extent, on such core industries as power, petroleum, fertilisers and machine tools. Thus, there is inter-dependence between agriculture and industry.

Government of India has launched a series of programmes/schemes in recent years to rejuvenate agriculture and improve farm income. Encouragement of FDI in the farm sector is a major policy initiative (Table 7.1).

7.4 FDI in Mining, Petroleum and Natural Gas

The metallurgical and mineral industries constitute the bedrock of industrial sector as they provide the basic raw materials for most of the industries. The development and management of mineral resources plays a major role in the industrial growth of a nation and its people at large. As minerals form the basis of modern industry in peace and in war, it is necessary to have a rational policy as regards their working and utilisation. The keynote of this policy should be conservation and economic working.

Table 7.1: FDI in Agriculture and Allied Sectors

Sector/Activity	Percent of equity/FDI Cap	Entry Route
1. Agriculture and Animal Husbandry (a) Floriculture, horticulture, and cultivation of vegetables and mushrooms under controlled conditions, (b) development and production of seeds and planting material, (c) animal husbandry (including breeding of dogs), pisciculture, aquaculture, under controlled conditions and (d) services related to agro and allied sectors. **Note:** Besides the above, FDI is not allowed in any other agricultural sector/activity	100%	Automatic
2. Plantation Sector (a) Tea sector including tea plantations, (b) coffee plantations, (c) rubber plantations, (d) cardamom plantations, (e) palm oil tree plantations and (f) olive oil tree plantations **Note:** Besides the above, FDI is not allowed in any other plantation sector/activity	100%	Automatic

Source: Government of India, Ministry of Commerce and Industry, Department for Promotion of Industry and Internal Trade (DPIIT), *Consolidated FDI Policy* (effective from October 15, 2020).

Minerals, being non-renewable resources of the country, require special attention so that these are exploited and utilised in an optimal manner. The role of mineral prospecting, exploration, mining and utilisation assumes importance in this context.

The petroleum sector dominates India's current energy use. This is one of the most vulnerable sectors in the Indian energy scenario. As an oil deficit country, India is dependent upon imports of the crude oil. India's oil reserves amount to 0.5 per cent of the global reserves. Due to the stagnating domestic production of crude oil, India imports approximately 85 percent of its oil needs, much of it from the Middle East. Its dependence on imported oil is growing steadily. FDI in mining and petroleum sectors is encouraged through a liberal investment policy (Table 7.2).

Table 7.2: FDI in Mining, Petroleum and Natural Gas

Sector/Activity	Percent of equity/FDI Cap	Entry Route
1. Mining		
A. Mining and exploration of metal and non-metal ores including diamond, gold, silver and precious ores but excluding titanium bearing minerals and its ores; subject to specified conditions.	100%	Automatic
B. Coal and lignite mining for captive consumption by power projects, iron and steel and cement units and other eligible activities. Setting up coal processing plants like washeries; subject to specified conditions.	100%	Automatic

contd...

C. Mining and mineral separation of titanium bearing minerals and ores, its value addition and integrated activities subject to specified conditions.	100%	Government
2. Petroleum and Natural Gas		
A. Exploration activities of oil and natural gas fields, and related activities subject to the existing sectoral policy and regulatory framework.	100%	Automatic
B. Petroleum refining by the Public Sector Undertakings (PSU), without any disinvestment or dilution of domestic equity in the existing PSUs.	49%	Automatic

Source: Same as for Table 7.1.

7.5 FDI in Defence Industry

Defence expenditure started increasing steadily after the Chinese aggression in 1962, and the Indo-Pak conflicts in 1965 and 1971. Defence expenditure, chiefly determined by the geo-political situation, is almost a committed expenditure.

In view of growing global tensions there is little scope for stabilisation much less reduction in defence expenditure. Defence expenditure is a sacred cow in India and any suggestion to control or reduce it is construed as almost unpatriotic. However, restraining defence expenditure should not be understood in terms of weakening defence preparedness. It simply means exploring the possibilities of achieving the existing level of defence preparedness at reduced costs.

Prime Minister Narendra Modi announced on May 12, 2020, the Aatmanirbhar Bharat Abhiyan which combined relief, policy reforms and fiscal and monetary measures to help businesses and individuals to cope with the situation created by COVID-19 pandemic. This programme also included a major opening up of coal, defence production, civil aviation, power, space, social infrastructure and atomic energy for private participation. List of weapons was notified for import ban.

Table 7.3 records conditions on FDI for manufacturing and defence sectors.

Table 7.3: FDI in Defence Sector

Sector/Activity	Percent of equity/FDI Cap	Entry Route
Defence Defence industry subject to industrial license under the Industries (Development and Regulation) Act, 1951 and manufacturing of small arms and ammunition under Arms Act, 1959.	100%	Automatic up to 74%. Government route beyond 74% wherever it is likely to result in access to modern technology or for other reasons to be recorded.

Source: Same as for Table 7.1.

7.6 FDI in Services Sector

Since the early 1990s, the growth process in India has been marked by a remarkable performance of services sector. The experience of developed countries suggests that growth of services sector followed the growth of industrial sector. However, India's experience in this regard is somewhat different. The sectoral shift in favour of services sector over the last two decades has taken place in the face of an almost stagnant share of industry and a reduced share of agriculture in GDP. In fact, it was the growth performance of the services sector during the 1990s which sustained the overall growth of the Indian economy, particularly in times of adverse agricultural shocks and industrial slowdown.

The expansion of services has not only been conducive for employment generation but also for better efficiency of the system and better quality of life. Caps and conditions on FDI in the services sector are listed in Table 7.4.

Table 7.4: FDI in Services Sector

Sector/Activity	Percent of equity/FDI Cap	Entry Route
1. Broadcasting		
A. Broadcasting Carriage Services		
Teleports, cable networks, mobile TV and other services.	100%	Automatic
B. Broadcasting Content Services		
Terrestrial broadcasting FM (FM Radio) and up-linking of news and current affairs TV channels	49%	Government
Up-linking of non-news and current affairs TV channels/down-linking of TV channels	100%	Automatic

contd...

2. Print Media		
A. Publishing of newspaper and periodicals dealing with news and current affairs B. Publication of Indian editions of foreign magazines dealing with news and current affairs	26%	Government
C. Publishing/printing of scientific and technical magazines/specialty journals/periodicals, subject to specified conditions. D. Publication of facsimile edition of foreign newspapers	100%	Government
3. Civil Aviation		
A. Airports		
• Greenfield projects	100%	Automatic
• Existing projects	100%	Automatic
B. Air Transport Services		
• Scheduled air transport service/domestic scheduled passenger airline. • Regional air transport service	100%	Automatic up to 49%. Government route beyond 49%. Automatic up to 100% for NRIs.
• Non-scheduled air transport service • Helicopter services/seaplane services requiring DGCA approval	100%	Automatic

contd...

C. Other Services under Civil Aviation Sector	100%	Automatic
4. Construction Development: Townships, Housing, Built-up Infrastructure	100%	Automatic
5. Industrial Parks: New and Existing	100%	Automatic
6. Satellites: Establishment and Operation	100%	Government
7. Private Security Agencies	74%	Automatic up to 49%. Government route beyond 49% and up to 74%
8. Telecom Services	100%	Automatic up to 49% Government route beyond 49%
9. Trading		
A. Cash and carry wholesale trading.	100%	Automatic
B. E-commerce activities	100%	Automatic
C. Single Brand Product Retail Trading	100%	Automatic
D. Multi Brand Retail Trading	51%	Government
E. Duty Free Shops	100%	Automatic
10. Railway Infrastructure		
Construction, operation and maintenance of high speed train projects, dedicated freight lines, mass rapid transport systems and others.	100%	Automatic

Source: Same as for Table 7.1.

7.7 FDI in Financial Services

Financial sector of an economy is a multi-faceted term. It refers to the whole gamut of legal and institutional arrangements, financial intermediaries, markets and instruments with both domestic and external dimensions.

A well-functioning financial system is a pre-requisite for the pursuit of economic growth with stability. The core function of a financial system is to facilitate smooth and efficient allocation of resources from savers to the ultimate users. The financial infrastructure contributes to the effective functioning of institutions and markets and thereby to stability. Hence, it serves as the foundation for adequate access to financial services and sustained financial development.

No major economy in the world today can be viewed in isolation from the rest of the world. Given the size and the growing magnitude of interaction—in terms of trade, services, and capital flows—and the greater openness to globalisation, India is in a different economic milieu today than it was two decades ago. India is virtually part of the world of globalised finance and is learning to walk, negotiating the strong currents, both positive and negative, generated by the forces of financial globalisation.

FDI in financial services is indicated in Table 7.5.

7.8 FDI in Pharmaceuticals

Pharmaceutical industry (including biotech) has done really well in establishing a global reputation for quality products. There is an opportunity for India to become *pharmacy of the world.* So far, pharma exports have been dominated by generics and prospects for expansion in this segment are good. Developed economies are facing fiscal problems and wherever public health is a major charge on the national exchequer, governments will have to rely upon high quality generics instead of patented or brand-named drugs. This is an opportunity India cannot miss. Table 7.6 shows liberal policy for FDI in the pharmaceutical industry

Table 7.5: FDI in Financial Services

Sector/Activity	Percent of equity/FDI Cap	Entry Route
1. Asset Reconstruction Companies	100%	Automatic
2. Banking–Private sector	74%	Automatic up to 49%. Government route beyond 49% and up to 74%.
3. Banking-Public Sector	20%	Government
4. Credit Information Companies (CIC).	100%	Automatic
5. Infrastructure Companies in Securities Markets		
Infrastructure companies in securities markets, namely, stock exchanges, depositories and clearing corporations, in compliance with SEBI Regulations.	49%	Automatic
6. Insurance		
Insurance company.	49%	Automatic
Insurance intermediaries	100%	Automatic
7. Pension Sector	49%	Automatic
8. Power Exchanges	49%	Automatic
9. White Label ATM Operations	100%	Automatic
10. Other Financial Services	100%	Automatic

Source: Same as for Table 7.1.

Table 7.6: FDI in Pharmaceuticals

Sector/Activity	Percent of equity/FDI Cap	Entry Route
Greenfield	100%	Automatic
Brownfield	100%	Automatic up to 74%. Government route beyond 74%

Source: Same as for Table 7.1.

8

Favourable Factors for FDI in India

Foreign direct investment (FDI) is an important source of non-debt finance and hence a factor in the economic development of a country. Apart from supplementing domestic investment, it brings with it internationally available technologies, managerial skills and practices, and new employment opportunities.

8.1 Why FDI is Important for India?

FDI plays an important role in the long-term economic development of a country. It is seen as a means to supplement domestic investment for achieving a higher level of economic growth. FDI benefits domestic industry as well as consumers in several ways:

1. Enhancing competitiveness of the domestic economy through transfer of technology.
2. Access to global managerial skills and practices.
3. Strengthening infrastructure and logistics.
4. Opening up export markets.
5. Providing backward and forward linkages.
6. Access to international quality goods and services.
7. Generating new employment opportunities.

In view of the foregoing advantages, the FDI policy has been constantly reviewed and necessary steps have been taken to make India a favourable destination for FDI. In fact, FDI is a strategic instrument of development policy.

8.2 World Investment Report, 2020 and India

World Investment Report is published every year by United Nations Conference on Trade and Development (UNCTAD). It supports policymakers by monitoring global and regional foreign direct investment (FDI) trends and documents national and international investment policy developments.

According to the *World Investment Report, 2020* of the United Nations Conference on Trade and Development (UNCTAD), India jumped from 12th spot in 2018 to 9th spot in 2019 on the list of global top 20 recipients of FDI. In other words, India was among the top 10 recipients of FDI. FDI inflows into India increased from US$ 44 billion in 2018 to US$ 51 billion in 2019.

As per the 2020 report, India's economy could prove the most resilient in South Asia notwithstanding the COVID-19 crisis. FDI to India has been on a long-term growth trend. India's large market will continue to attract market-seeking investments in the country. India's most sought-after industries, which include professional services and the digital enterprises, could see a faster rebound as global venture firms and technology companies continue to show interest in India's market through acquisitions.

Although India has been a preferred destination for foreign investors for long, the recent upsurge in flow of funds into the country is quite remarkable and encouraging.

There are several good reasons for investing in India. Preference of foreign investors for India is indicated by a host of factors: India is the fifth largest economy in the world which offers a large reservoir of skilled manpower, infrastructure and logistic facilities, a single nationwide indirect tax (GST), a robust and reliable financial system, and where English is the preferred language of business.

8.3 Large and Expanding Size of the Market

Foreign investors' confidence lies in the large and expanding consumer market in India and the future of its digital economy.

India is the fifth largest economy in the world (after US, China, Japan and Germany). With an estimated population of 130 crore (1.3 billion), it is the second most populous country in the world (after China). According to a study published in *Lancet* journal (July 2020), India's population would peak at 160 crore (1.6 billion) in 2048. The country will have the world's largest working-age population of 57.8 crore (578 million) by 2100.

India has an estimated middle class of 40 crore (400 million) people who are the mainstay of consumption expenditure. In view of the focus of present government on rural areas and farmers, rural India is also emerging as a promising market for all types of consumer goods, even branded ones.

India is strategically located with easy access to markets of Bangladesh, Nepal, Pakistan, Sri Lanka and Myanmar.

According to a global study of 75 countries, the data for which was jointly released on July 16, 2020 by United Nations Development Program (UNDP) and Oxford Poverty and Human Development Initiative (OPHI), as many as 27 crore (270 million) people in India were lifted out of multi-dimensional poverty between 2005-06 and 2015-16. India showed the largest reduction in the number of poor. The multi-dimensional poverty index (MPI), developed by OPHI, included, apart from income, access to safe water, education, electricity, food and six other indicators.

Governments in India (Centre and States) spend massively on administration, development programmes and welfare schemes aimed at disadvantages sections of society. Central Government alone showed total expenditure of ₹ 24 lakh crore in the budget for 2020-21 presented to the Parliament on February 1, 2020 by the Finance Minister Nirmala Sitharaman.

8.4 US and Western World's Disenchantment with China

Post-COVID, the world is hostile towards China, the epicentre of coronavirus. Moreover, rising US-China tensions in the South China Sea are scaring away global corporate giants, especially those based in the US, from a potentially troubled and contentious region. The pandemic has led several companies to de-couple their supply chains from China to mitigate risks arising out of natural and geopolitical disturbances.

In such a scenario, economic and financial distancing from China may be a policy prescription not only for US and its Western allies, but also for other countries. US and Western companies, at the behest of their governments, are planning to shift their manufacturing units and withdraw investment from China. China's reputation is at its lowest ebb after the pandemic. In the October 13, 2020 voting in the 193-member UN general Assembly, China secured 139 votes (as against 180 three years ago) to win a seat on the UN Humam Rights Council

Owing to reasons stated above, transnational companies and other big firms are turning away from China and looking at India as the next best location for their business activities.

India can be their next best destination provided it readies itself to leverage this opportunity. It underscores the need to make India more business-friendly for prospective foreign investors. This requires government incentives, Centre-State co-ordination, and joint venture offers from Indian corporates. Although India has jumped on the ease-of-doing-business rank in recent years, it is yet to break into the top 50 countries.

In the recent past, many companies have withdrawn from China and relocated themselves in Taiwan, Thailand, Vietnam, and India. For example, the German shoe brand, Von Wellx, recently (October 2020) shifted its manufacturing units from China to Agra in Uttar Pradesh (UP). The German brand has collaborated with an Indian company, Iatric Industries Group, to shift its manufacturing units to Agra's Exports Promotion Industrial Park. It is noteworthy that UP has also taken a big leap in the Ease of Doing Business rankings among the states and is currently in the second position after Andhra Pradesh which tops the list.

8.5 Ease of Doing Business

In recent years, India has climbed the ranks on many world

indices of economic efficiency and performance. According to the recent *Doing Business Reports* of World Bank, India has consistently and significantly improved its ranking in recent years from 142 in 2015 to 130 in 2017, to 100 in 2018, to 77 in 2019 and to 63 in 2020, a jump of 79 spots over the period from 2015 to 2020.

The present Central Government led by Prime Minister Narendra Modi has made ease of doing business a clear area of focus. Likewise, state governments are also taking business facilitation measures to attract investment and enterprise to their respective states. While the incentive package varies from state to state depending upon their investment priorities, some common features are discernible. These include development of industrial estates, removing artificial barriers within the state, decentralisation of decision-making, time-bound clearance of projects, investment subsidy, and power tariff concessions.

This competitive federalism offers a powerful framework within which India is reforming its business environment. Resultantly, India is being viewed by global investors as the economic power house of the future.

8.6 Digital Revolution

The Government of India has taken policy decision to encourage electronic transactions and has, in this regard, announced a number of incentives. Technology, competition, and benchmarking to the best international practices are the driving force of India's developmental efforts. Digital technology is expanding in various sectors of the Indian economy, including money, banking, finance, taxation, e-commerce, agriculture, rural development, and governance.

According to a 2018 survey by The Economist Intelligence Unit, commissioned by payments company Visa, India was taking rapid strides in advancing government e-payments capabilities and was one of the top-performing countries in terms of citizen-to-government (C2G), business-to-government (B2G) and government-to-business (G2B) transactions. India got the top ranking on B2G and G2B, and came third on C2G jointly with Argentina. In a 73-country survey, India's overall ranking on government's adoption of e-payments moved up to 28th in 2018, from 36th in 2011. According to the survey, India could further improve its standing by focusing on expanding access to digital infrastructure, investing in socio-economic development, and promoting a healthy, competitive market.

In the World Digital Competitiveness Ranking prepared by the International Institute for Management Development, Lausanne (Switzerland) for 63 economies, India moved up four places to 44th rank in 2019 as compared to 48th rank in 2018. Its position in 2019 improved overall in all factors including knowledge, technology and future readiness in exploring more digital technologies. India's biggest improvement in 2019 was in the technology sub-factor level, where it held first position in telecommunications investment.

8.7 Well-managed Public Finances

In India, Fiscal Responsibility and Budget Management (FRBM) Act, 2003 ensures the conduct of transparent, prudent and accountable fiscal policy on the part of the government. It imposes limits on fiscal deficit and government debt.

Goods and services tax (GST), launched on July 1, 2017, is an all-India unified, uniform, harmonized and technology-based indirect tax system. Implementation of GST in a large and complex federal system of India, was perhaps unprecedented in modern global tax history. Income tax, levied by the central government, is the main source of direct tax revenue. It is levied on individuals and companies at moderate rates. Administration of the tax is completely digitized including e-filing of returns, e-assessment, e-payment of tax and digital signatures.

India is a federal polity. Apart from the central government, there are 28 states and 8 union territories. In a spirit of co-operative federalism, the centre and the state governments are guided by the broader national concerns of using the available resources for the benefit of the people. Co-operative federalism has encouraged the governments at different levels to take advantage of a large national market, diverse and rich natural resources and the potential of human capabilities in all parts of the country and from all sections of the society for building a prosperous nation.

8.8 Robust and Resilient Financial System

India with its uniquely rich payment ecosystem is now emerging as a global leader in innovative payment systems. The growth of financial services in India has largely been led by commercial banks. Reserve Bank of India (RBI) provided the initial thrust and support for digital payments infrastructure and systems. Non-banks have also entered the market and expanded the range of payment services available to clients backed by their strength in technology and customer-centric innovation.

Among the many stock exchanges in India, Bombay Stock Exchange (BSE) and the National Stock Exchange (NSE) are the most important in terms of providing nation-wide services to investors. Equity trading is most active in these two competing stock exchanges. Trading infrastructure in the stock exchanges is anonymous and order-driven, wherein all orders from market participants are matched with respect to strike price/time priority. The Indian capital market is significant in terms of its degree of development, its volume of trading and the quality of its automated trading and settlement.

Trading in derivatives—such as stock index futures, stock index options and futures and options in individual stocks—is in place to provide hedging options to the investors and to improve *price discovery* mechanism in the market. Derivative instruments are available in the foreign exchange market, the money market and the equity market. In the foreign exchange market, the instruments are available in the form of currency forwards, swaps and forward rate agreements (FRAs) and rupee options.

Securities and Exchange Board of India (SEBI), as an

autonomous and independent statutory body, oversees the development of the securities market. Its objectives include: (a) regulation of the securities market activities, (b) protection of the interests of investors in securities, (c) prevention of malpractices and (d) implementation of the code of conduct for intermediaries. SEBI prohibits fraudulent and unfair trade practices, including insider trading. It also regulates substantial acquisition of shares and takeovers. In order to ensure protection of investors and to safeguard the integrity of the markets, there is a comprehensive surveillance system. Stock exchanges are the primary targets for detection of market manipulation, price rigging and other regulatory breaches regarding capital market functioning.

It may be recalled that India's financial sector escaped almost unscathed during the unprecedented financial crisis of 2007-08 when economies of developed countries went topsy-turvy and financial giants, including Lehman Brothers, collapsed like a house of cards.

India's financial institutions, particularly banks, and financial markets continued to function normally even during successive nationwide lockdowns in the wake of COVID-19.

8.9 Strong and Diversified Industrial, Infrastructural and Logistics Base

India has established a strong and diversified manufacturing base for the production of a wide variety of basic and capital goods to meet the requirements of various sectors including heavy electricals, power generation and transmission, process equipment, automobiles, ships, mining, chemicals, and crude oil refining. There is a considerable potential for growth which, in a globalized world economy, is based on improving productivity and competitiveness. Innovation and adoption of new technologies are the key factors in competitiveness. In the Indian context, the opening up of the economy and the subsequent entry of international players has substantially enhanced the need for production of goods and services matching international standards.

India has systematically rolled out a public-private-partnership (PPP) programme for the delivery of high-priority public utilities and infrastructure and developed what is perhaps one of the largest PPP programmes in the world. Government is promoting PPP as an effective tool for bringing private sector efficiencies in the creation of economic and social infrastructure assets and for delivery of quality public services. Traditionally, infrastructure development was engineered through the public sector. However, in the face of scarcity of public resources and the need to shift these into health and education, efforts have been made to induct private participation in the development of infrastructure. These efforts have met with a fair degree of success.

Recognizing its importance for exports and growth, the government has included logistics in the harmonized master list of the infrastructure sub-sector. This has eased access to credit and simplified the approval process for building infrastructure in the sector.

The Logistics Division in the Department of Commerce, Ministry of Commerce and Industry, Government of India was created on July 7, 2017. The Division has been given the mandate to develop an Action Plan for the integrated development of the logistics sector in the country, by way of policy changes, improvement in existing procedures, identification of bottlenecks and gaps and introduction of technology in this sector.

8.10 Rising Innovations Ranking

India, which was ranked at 81st place in the 2015 Global Innovation Index (GII) published by the World Intellectual Property Organization (WIPO), jumped to 66th spot in 2016, 60th in 2017, 57th in 2018, 52nd in 2019 and 48th in 2020. Thus, India jumped 33 notches in five years and made it to the top 50 among 131 countries ranked on the GII.

Similarly, India, for the first time, made its place on the list of

60 countries for which data was published in the Bloomberg Innovation Index, 2019 report. As a debutant, India occupied 54th position in the index prepared and published by Bloomberg, a New York-based media firm.

8.11 Start-up Hub

Global Start-up Ecosystem Report (GSER), 2020, released on June 25, 2020, by Start-up Genome and Global Entrepreneurship Network (GEN) is the world's most comprehensive and widely-read research on start-up ecosystems. Start-up Genome is the world-leading policy advisory and research organization for governments and public-private-partnerships committed to accelerating the success of their start-up ecosystem. Start-up Genome, headquartered in California, has been tracking the growth of start-up ecosystems around the world since 2012. GEN works to build smarter entrepreneurial ecosystems in every national economy, operating a platform of projects and programmes in 170 countries aimed at making it easier for anyone, anywhere to start and scale a business.

GSER ranks the top 140 start-up ecosystems from an assessment of several hundreds. It ranks the top ecosystems by a number of metrices including performance, funding, connectedness, talent and knowledge. The report analyses cities around the world where early stage start-ups have the best shot at building global success.

The ranking for 2020 was topped by Silicon Valley in California, USA.

Two Indian cities made it to the top 40 of the world's most *favourable ecosystems* to build a globally successful start-up. Bengaluru was ranked 26th and Delhi 36th in the report.

Mumbai (India) topped the list of *emerging ecosystems* (Table 8.1).

8.12 Realistic Exchange Rate and Sufficient Foreign Exchange Reserves

The distinct improvement in the external sector of India has enabled a progressive liberalization of the exchange and payments regime. The exchange rate is market-determined. Exchange rate management is flexible without fixed or pre-announced targets or bands, with interventions primarily to ensure orderly market conditions. India's exchange rate policy is perceived to be realistic and the exchange rate is among the least volatile in emerging market economies.

Table 8.1: Top Ten Emerging Start-up Ecosystems in the World

Rank	City	Country	Rank	City	Country
1.	Mumbai	India	6.	Barcelona (tie)	Spain
2.	Jakarta	Indonesia	6.	Madrid (tie)	Spain
3.	Zurich	Switzerland	8.	Philadelphia	USA
4.	Helsinki	Finland	9.	Manchester-Liverpool	UK
5.	Guangzhou	China	10.	Research Triangle	USA

Source: *The Global Start-up Ecosystem Report (GSER) 2020,* p. 44.

As per *Weekly Statistical Supplement* of RBI published on July 23, 2021, India's total foreign exchange reserves stood at US$ 612 billion as on July 16, 2021, the highest ever.

India's robust and burgeoning foreign exchange reserves guarantee timely payment for repatriation of profits and portfolio outflows. They provide confidence in the country's ability to manage balance of payments. These reserves indicate an import cover of about 1 year as against the benchmark of 3 months of International Monetary Fund (IMF).

India's comfortable foreign exchange reserves provide confidence in the country's ability to manage balance of payments. Foreign exchange reserves act as the first line of defence for India in case of economic emergency.

These reserves facilitate external trade and payment and promote orderly development and maintenance of the foreign exchange market. It may be recalled that India's foreign exchange reserves had dipped to as low as US$ 5 billion in early 1991 which prompted the then Prime Minister Narsimha Rao to introduce economic reforms in India.

Foreign exchange reserves have been increasing in recent years due to rise in foreign direct investment (FDI) and also foreign portfolio investment. Foreign investors have acquired stakes in several Indian companies in recently. Fall in international crude oil prices in the wake of Covid-19 has brought down oil import bill significantly, saving precious foreign exchange. Foreign exchange reserves are around 15 percent of GDP.

8.13 Political Stability and Cordial International Relations

Political stability of a country is an important driver of technological advancement. Availability of foreign funds and venture capital to finance technological development is relatively easy for politically stable economies. In contrast, in economies that are high in political instability, financing is more challenging.

Political stability is an asset for India. The present government got a massive mandate in 2019 to rule for 5 years. India is the largest democracy in the world with independent judiciary and a firebrand media. The Constitution of India guarantees freedom of expression. English is the preferred business language.

India has maintained cordial relations with countries of the world. On June 18, 2020, India was elected non-permanent member of the UN Security Council (UNSC) for the eighth time for a two-year term. India won 184 of the 192 votes cast in the elections for five non-permanent UNSC seats. In 2022, India will host the G-20, the world's most influential multilateral economic forum.

Currently, there are more than 6,700 troops and police from India who have been deployed to UN peacekeeping missions, the fourth highest amongst troop-contributing countries. More than 160 Indian peacekeepers have paid the ultimate price in service to peace, losing their lives serving under the UN flag.

On February 17, 2021, India gifted 2 lakh doses of COVID

vaccine for UN peacekeepers, a gesture which was highly appreciated by UN Secretary General Antonio Guterres.

A victim of terrorist attacks from neighbouring Pakistan, India is playing a leading role in containing international terrorism by curbing terror funding and training.

To sum up, the far reaching and sweeping economic reforms undertaken since 1991 have unleashed the enormous growth potential of the Indian economy. There has been a rapid, yet calibrated, move towards deregulation and liberalisation, which has resulted in India becoming a favourite destination for foreign investment. The mood is upbeat and the signals strong. Undoubtedly, India has emerged as one of the most vibrant and dynamic developing economies of the world.

In the wake of economic liberalisation policy initiated in 1991, the Government of India has taken several measures to encourage foreign investment, both direct and portfolio, in almost all sectors of the economy. However, the emphasis has been on foreign direct investment (FDI) inflows in the: (a) development of infrastructure, (b) technological upgradation of Indian industry, (c) projects having the potential for creating employment opportunities on a large scale, and (d) setting up special economic zones and establishing manufacturing units therein. With a vast reservoir of skilled and cost-effective manpower, India is now recognized as one of the most attractive investment destinations by reputed international rating organisations.

Promotion of foreign direct investment forms an integral part of India's economic policies. The role of foreign direct investment in accelerating economic growth is by way of infusion of capital, technology and modern management practices. Government has put in place a liberal and transparent foreign investment regime where most activities are opened to foreign investment on automatic route without any limit on the extent of foreign ownership.

The Government, keen to promote investment in the country, has radically simplified and rationalised polices, procedures and regulatory aspects. Foreign investment is welcome in almost all sectors, expect those of strategic concern (defence and atomic energy).

Global community, including businesses and foreign governments, has started taking note of India's rise and recognizing opportunities for investments and enterprise. India's massive workforce and democratic functioning suggest that the future of labour-intensive industry lies here.

9

Foreign Portfolio Investment

Portfolio investment occurs when individual investors invest, mostly through stockbrokers, in stocks of foreign companies in foreign land in search of profit opportunities. In India, foreign portfolio investor (FPI) means a person registered in accordance with the provisions of Securities and Exchange Board of India (SEBI) (Foreign Portfolio Investors) Regulations, 2014, as amended from time to time. Similarly, foreign institutional investor (FII) means an entity established or incorporated outside India which proposes to make investment in India and which is registered as a FII in accordance with the Securities and Exchange Board of India (SEBI) (Foreign Institutional Investor) Regulations, 1995.

Institutional investors are specialised financial intermediaries managing savings collectively on behalf of investors, especially small investors, towards specific objectives in terms of risk, returns, and maturity of claims.

One of the major forces changing the face and structure of international capital markets since 1990s has been the flow of cross-border portfolio investments—especially by foreign institutional investors (FIIs), from developed countries to the developing countries. Portfolio investors provide institutional character to the capital markets, flavoured by highly intensive research and diversified investments. FII investments inject global liquidity into the markets, raise the price-earning ratio and thus reduce the cost of capital. From the perspective of FIIs, investments in various countries provide a measure of portfolio diversification and hedging as also to take advantage of arbitrage opportunities.

FIIs make investments in various countries to provide a measure of portfolio diversification and hedging to their assets.

The forces driving the recent change in the investment portfolio of FIIs, as reflected in the growing emphasis on equities of emerging market economies, include *inter alia*: (a) increased accessibility of these markets after liberalisation, (b) improved marketability, (c) fewer problems relating to thin trading and (d) improved macroeconomic fundamentals of these countries.

9.1 Advantages of Portfolio Investment Inflows

Following are the chief advantages of having investments by foreign institutional investors (FIIs).

9.1.1 Improvement in Corporate Capital Structure: FIIs are well-known for a greater appetite for equity than debt in their asset structure. Thus, opening up the economy to FIIs is in line with the accepted preference for non-debt creating foreign inflows over foreign debt. Furthermore, because of this preference for equities over bonds, FIIs can help in compressing the yield-differential between equity and bonds and improve corporate capital structure.

9.1.2 Competition in Financial Markets: Institutional investors promote financial innovation and development of hedging instruments. Institutions, for example, because of their interest in hedging risks, are known to have contributed to the development of zero-coupon bonds and index futures. FIIs, as professional bodies of asset managers and financial analysts, not only enhance competition in financial markets, but also improve the alignment of asset prices to fundamentals.

Institutions in general and FIIs in particular are known to have good information and low transaction costs. By aligning asset prices closer to fundamentals, they stabilize markets. Fundamentals are known to be sluggish in their movements. Thus, if prices are aligned to fundamentals, they should be as stable as the fundamentals themselves. Furthermore, FIIs with a variety of risk-return preferences also help in dampening volatility.

9.1.3 Enhanced Efficiency in Capital Markets: FIIs as

professional bodies of asset managers and financial analysts enhance competition and efficiency of financial markets. Equity market development aids economic development. By increasing the availability of riskier long-term capital for projects, FIIs can help in the process of economic development.

9.1.4 Improvement in Corporate Governance: Good corporate governance is essential to overcome the principal-agent problem between shareholders and management. Information asymmetries and incomplete contracts between shareholders and management are at the root of the agency costs. Bad corporate governance makes equity finance a costly option.

FIIs contribute to better understanding of operations and improve corporate governance of firms. Institutions are known for challenging excessive executive compensation, and removing under performing managers. There is some evidence that institutionalization increases dividend payouts, and enhances productivity growth.

9.2 Disadvantages of Portfolio Investment Inflows

Among others, the two common apprehensions about FIIs inflows are the fear of management takeovers and potential capital outflows.

9.2.1 Management Control: FIIs act as agents on behalf of their principals as financial investors maximising returns. There are domestic laws that effectively prohibit institutional investors from taking management control. In India, all takeovers are governed by SEBI's Substantial Acquisition of Shares and Takeovers Regulations, 1997, and sub-accounts of FIIs are deemed to be *persons acting in concert* with other persons in the same category unless the contrary is established. In addition, reporting requirements have been imposed on FIIs and currently *participatory notes* cannot be issued to unregulated entities abroad.

9.2.2 Volatility of Portfolio Flows: FIIs inflows are popularly described as *hot money* because of the herd behaviour and potential for large capital outflows. Herd behaviour means FIIs trying to either only buy or only sell at the same time, particularly at times of market stress. Value at risk models followed by FIIs may destabilise markets by leading to simultaneous sale by various FIIs. Extrapolative expectations or trend chasing, rather than focusing on fundamentals, can lead to destabilization.

It has been argued that under the process of globalisation, highly diversified investors participate in cross-border movement of capital. Such investors pay little attention to economic fundamentals and in the presence of asymmetric information they resort to herd behaviour, which results in volatility of international capital flows. Such a view has, however, been challenged and it has been argued that there is high level of substitutability between various forms of foreign capital.

Countries with modest growth potentials and semi-developed financial market infrastructure are most vulnerable to reversal of portfolio investment flows. Existence of large asymmetry of information in such countries can lead to sharp changes in portfolio and private debt flows in the face of even a slight change in investor perception about the health of the recipient economy. This type of volatility is, however, not limited to portfolio flows. Even external commercial borrowings, in the form of bank borrowing or bond financing, show similar patterns.

9.2.3 Pro-cyclical: The most important disadvantage of FII flows is that it tends to be pro-cyclical, in the sense that it comes in when the balance of payments (BOP) position is seen to be strong and goes out when the BOP position is expected to weaken. Thus, it accentuates the direction of movement of the BOP, which can cause serious problems in macroeconomic management. In the case of countries like India, where the foreign exchange markets are very thin as compared to the international financial market, a free FII regime carries the danger of speculative movements, which can lead to serious disruption in the economy.

9.2.4 Hedge Funds: Hedge funds are another source of

concern which (unlike pension funds, life insurance companies and mutual funds) engage in short-term trading, take short positions and borrow more aggressively.

Mexican crisis and more recently the East Asian crisis have highlighted the downside risks of such flows. The downside risks include political risk, currency risk, problems associated with low liquidity and volatility on returns. Cross-country studies indicate that reversal of portfolio flows could be disorderly and result in substantial economic hardship for developing countries.

9.3 Liberalisation of Portfolio Investment Flows into India

Prior to 1992, only non-resident Indians (NRIs) and overseas corporate bodies (OCBs) were allowed to undertake portfolio investment in India. In line with the recommendations of the High Level Committee on Balance of Payments (Chairman: C. Rangarajan), FIIs were allowed to invest in the Indian debt and equity market. FII investments first started flowing into India in 1993. Portfolio investment inflows have since then been substantial.

9.3.1 Investments by FIIs: India embarked on a gradual shift towards capital account convertibility with the launch of the reforms in the early 1990s. Although foreign natural persons—except NRIs—are prohibited from investing in financial assets, such investments are permitted by FIIs and Overseas Corporate Bodies (OCBs) with suitable restrictions. From September 14, 1992, FIIs were allowed to invest in all the securities traded on the primary and secondary markets, including shares, debentures and warrants issued by companies which were listed or were to be listed on the stock exchanges in India and in the schemes floated by domestic mutual funds. Funds invested by FIIs must have at least 50 participants with no one holding more than 5 percent to ensure a broad base and preventing such investment acting as a camouflage for individual investment in the nature of FDI and requiring Government approval.

The idea of allowing FIIs was that they were broad-based, diversified funds, leaving out individual foreign investors and foreign companies. The only exceptions were the NRI and OCB portfolio investments through the secondary market, which were subject to individual ceilings of 5 percent to prevent a possible *takeover*. Individuals were left out because of the difficulties in checking on their antecedents, and of their lack of expertise in market matters and relatively short-term perspective. OCB investments through the portfolio route were banned in November 2001.

During 1992-93, Government allowed reputed FIIs including pension funds, mutual funds, asset management companies, investment trusts nominee companies and incorporated or institutional portfolio managers to invest in the Indian capital market subject to the condition that they registered with the Securities and Exchange Board of India (SEBI) and obtained RBI approval under FERA.

In 1996-97, the guidelines for investment by FIIs were further liberalised. The limit of investment for an individual FII was raised from 5 percent to 10 percent subject, however, to the aggregate limit of 24 percent for all FIIs. The FIIs were also allowed to invest in unlisted companies in the same manner as they were allowed to invest in listed companies. FII investments in debt securities of companies as 100 percent debt funds were allowed subject to certain guidelines. FIIs were also allowed to invest in the gilt-edged government securities with the framework of guidelines. FIIs were also allowed to invest in the gilt-edged government securities within the framework of guidelines, and proprietary funds have been allowed to invest in the country through the FII route.

As a follow up of the announcement made in the Union Budget 1997-98, aggregate investment ceilings for FIIs and non-resident Indians (including OCBs) were increased up to 30 percent subject to approval by the company's shareholders. Guidelines for foreign investment in preference shares issued by the Indian companies were also issued. These provided greater flexibility to Indian corporations in using preference shares as a form of financing. FIIs were also permitted to purchase/sell Treasury Bills within the overall approved debt ceilings.

A number of liberalization measures were taken in 1998-99 to promote portfolio foreign investment. In order to avoid NRIs being crowded out by FIIs, the aggregate ceiling for investment in a company by all NRIs/PIOs/OCBs through stock exchanges was made separate and exclusive of the investment ceiling available for FIIs. In addition, the aggregate investment ceiling for NRIs/PIOs/OCBs was raised from 5 percent to 10 percent of the paid-up capital of a company. In the case of listed Indian companies, the ceiling was raised to 24 percent of the paid-up capital under a general body resolution. Also, the investment limit by a single NRI/PIO/OCB was enhanced from 1 percent to 5 percent of the paid up capital. Policy pertaining to investment in unlisted companies was liberalised. NRIs/PIOs/OCBs were permitted to invest in unlisted companies.

FIIs were allowed to purchase and sell Government Securities and Treasury Bills within overall approved debt ceilings. To facilitate better risk management by investors, authorised dealers were permitted to provide forward cover to FIIs in respect of their fresh equity investments in India. Moreover, transactions among FIIs with respect to Indian stocks were no longer required post-facto conformation from the RBI. Also, 100 percent FII debt funds were permitted to invest in unlisted debt securities of Indian companies.

In March 1999, the RBI issued a notification granting general permission to mutual funds for issuing units to NRIs/PIOs/OCBs subject to certain specified norms, thereby dispensing with the existing procedure of obtaining prior permission. In addition, approval procedures were simplified by the RBI in respect of NRIs/PIOs/OCBs by granting them general permission in lieu of case by case approval procedure in a large number of areas. This included acceptance of deposits by Indian companies, investment in Air Taxi operations, sale of shares in stock exchanges, transfer of shares in stock exchanges, transfer of share/bonds/debentures and immovable properly to charitable trusts/organisations in India as gift, raising of loans by resident individuals/proprietorship concerns on non-repatriable basis, issue of Commercial Papers by Indian companies to NRIs etc.

In 1999-2000, with a view to expand the FIIs category, the Government permitted foreign corporates and high net worth individuals to invest through SEBI registered FIIs. Such investments were subject to a sub-limit of 5 percent within the aggregate limit for FII portfolio investments of 24 percent in a single company. Government also permitted SEBI registered domestic fund managers to manage foreign funds for investment in the Indian capital market through the portfolio investment route provided the funds were channelled through internationally recognised financial institutions and subject to the reporting requirements as applicable to FIIs.

In 2000-01, FIIs were permitted greater leverage in the primary/secondary markets by allowing enhancement of the aggregate FII investment ceiling in the issued and paid-up capital of Indian companies from the normal ceiling of 24 percent to 40 percent subject to prescribed procedures. The list of activities of non-banking financial companies (NBFCs) eligible for foreign equity investment was increased to 18 with the addition of micro-credit/rural credit. Foreign investment guidelines for NBFCs were amended for providing a minimum capitalisation norm of US$ 0.5 million for activities, which were not fund-based or consultative in nature, irrespective of the foreign equity participation level. The provision applied to investment advisory services, credit reference and rating agencies, financial consultancy, foreign exchange broking and money changing. Permission was granted to holding companies in NBFC activities with minimum capital of US$ 5 million, subject to specific conditions of disinvestment.

In order to provide stimulus to the growth of the venture capital industry in India, SEBI was made the single point nodal agency for registration of both domestic and overseas venture capital funds. Venture capital companies/funds were allowed to invest through the automatic route, subject to SEBI regulations and sector specific caps on FDI.

In February 2000, the FII regulations were amended to permit foreign corporates and high net worth individuals to also invest as sub-accounts of SEBI-registered FIIs. Foreign corporates and high net worth individuals fall outside the category of diversified investors. FIIs were also permitted to seek SEBI registration in respect of sub-accounts for their clients under the regulations. [1]

While initially FIIs were permitted to manage the sub-account of clients, the domestic portfolio managers or domestic asset management companies were also allowed to manage the funds of such sub-accounts and also to make application on behalf of such sub-accounts. Such sub-accounts could be an institution, or a fund, or a portfolio established or incorporated outside India, or a broad-based fund, or a proprietary fund, or even a foreign corporate or individual. So, in practice there are common categories of entities, which could be registered as both FIIs and sub-accounts. However, investment into a sub-account is to be made either by FIIs, or by domestic portfolio manager or asset management company, and not by itself directly.

In view of the concerns of some unregulated entities taking positions in the stock market through the mechanism of participatory notes (PNs) issued by FIIs, the issue was examined by the Ministry of Finance in consultation with RBI and SEBI. Following these consultations, in January 2004, SEBI stipulated that PNs are not to be issued to any non-regulated entity, and the principle of *know your clients* may be strictly adhered to. SEBI has indicated that the existing non-eligible PNs, would be permitted to expire or to be wound-down on maturity, or within a period of 5 years, whichever is earlier. Besides, reporting requirement on a regular basis has been imposed on all the FIIs.

In his 2011-12 budget speech, the Finance Minister further liberalized the portfolio investment route. He announced, "Currently, only FIIs and sub-accounts registered with the SEBI and NRIs are allowed to invest in mutual fund schemes. To liberalise the portfolio investment route, it has been decided to permit SEBI registered Mutual Funds to accept subscriptions from foreign investors who meet the KYC requirements for equity schemes. This would enable Indian mutual funds to have direct access to foreign investors and widen the class of foreign investors in Indian equity market". [2]

9.3.2 Equity Capital from Foreign Sources by Indian Corporates: Indian corporates are also allowed to access equity capital from foreign sources in the form of ADR/GDR and Euro issues. Policies on international offerings on ADRs/GDRs have been liberalised substantially and corporates are allowed to raise funds by way of ADRs/GDRs under automatic route, subject to specified guidelines.

Two-way fungibility in ADR/GDR issues of Indian companies has been introduced under which investors in India can purchase shares and deposit them with an Indian custodian for issue of ADRs/GDRs by the overseas depository to the extent of the ADRs/GDRs converted into underlying shares.

Indian corporate sector has been encouraged to access global capital markets through GDRs:

1. Foreign investors can invest in Indian companies through the GDR route without any lock-in period.
2. These receipts can be listed on any of the overseas stock exchanges and denominated in any convertible foreign currency. However, the underlying shares are denominated in Indian Rupees.
3. Private placement with US investors is also permissible in accordance with the US Securities Act.
4. Short-term capital gains are taxable at the rate of 65 percent along with business income.
5. Long-term capital gains (computed on holdings for more than 12 months) are taxable at the rate of 10 percent.

Guidelines for Euro-issues were liberalised in June 1996. The requirement of consistently good record of performance for 3 years was relaxed for companies wanting to raise GDRs or foreign currency convertible bonds (FCCBs) for financing investment in infrastructure. Restrictions on the number of issues that can be floated by an individual company or a group of companies during a financial year have been withdrawn. Earlier norms regarding end-uses of GDRs have been relaxed to include financing of import of capital goods, capital expenditure including domestic purchase/installation of plant, equipment and building, investments in software development, prepayments scheme entailing repayment of earlier external borrowings, investments abroad where these have been approved by competent authorities, and equity investment in joint ventures (JVs)/wholly-owned subsidiaries (WOs) in India. A company raising GDRs can use the proceeds up to the extent of 25 percent for the purpose of meeting working capital requirements and general corporate restructuring.

Furthermore, banks, financial institutions and non-banking finance companies registered with the RBI may raise GDRs without making reference to any end-uses. However, investment in the stock market and real estate is not permitted out of GDR proceeds.

GDR/ADR guidelines were further liberalised in 1998-99. Unlisted companies were permitted to float Euro issues under certain conditions. All end-use restrictions on GDR/ADR issues proceeds were removed, except the prevailing restrictions on investment in stock markets and real estate. The 90-day validity period for final approvals of GDR/ADR issues was withdrawn and final approval was continued to be valid, thereby imparting greater flexibility to issuing companies regarding the timing of issues. Indian companies were permitted to issue GDRs/ADRs in the case of bonus or right issue of shares, or on genuine business reorganisations. The companies, however, in all such cases, were required to get approval from the Department of Economic Affairs, Ministry of Finance, Government of India for the issue of GDRs/ADRs.

Considering the enhanced opportunities of Indian software companies for expanding globally, operational norms—governing their overseas investments and mode of financing acquisition of overseas software companies—were issued through a notification by the Ministry of Finance. It permitted Indian software companies, which were listed in foreign exchanges and had already floated ADR/GDR issues, to acquire foreign software companies and issue ADRs/GDRs without reference to the Government of India or the RBI up to the value limit of US$ 100 million. For acquisitions beyond US$ 100 million, proposals required examination by a Special Composite Committee in the RBI.

With a view to further liberalise the operational guidelines for ADR/GDR issues, it was decided to dispense with the track record scrutiny process for ADR/GDR issues and the two-stage approval by the Ministry of Finance. Indian companies were allowed to access the ADR/GDR markets through an automatic route without the prior approval of the Ministry of Finance subject to the specified norms and post-issue reporting requirement.

Furthermore, overseas business acquisitions through the ADR/GDR route were permitted under the automatic and simplified approval mechanism for Indian companies engaged in: (a) information technology and entertainment software; (b) pharmaceuticals; (c) biotechnology and (d) any other sector as notified by the Government from time to time. The automatic approvals was made subject to conditions of previous listing, conformation to FDI policy and limiting of transactions to US$ 100 million or ten times the export earnings during the preceding financial year. Indian companies, engaged in IT software and IT services, were permitted to issue ADR/GDR linked stock options to permanent employees (including Indian and overseas working directors) of its subsidiary companies incorporated in India or outside and engaged in IT software and IT services.

In order to encourage greater skill development in knowledge-based Indian firms, Indian companies engaged in information technology and entertainment software, pharmaceuticals, biotechnology, and any other activities within the knowledge-based sector were permitted to issue ESOPs (employees' stock options) to their permanent employees. The liberalised norms for ESOPs were extended to multi-product diversified companies subject to specific conditions.

Government continued its policy of liberalising the guidelines for issue of GDRs/ADRs in a phased manner. The initiatives taken in 2001-02 included the following:

1. As a follow up of the announcement in the Budget for 2001-02, Indian companies were permitted to list in foreign stock exchanges by sponsoring ADR/GDR issues with overseas depository against shares held by its shareholders subject to prescribed conditions.
2. All companies that had made an ADR/GDR issue earlier and listed abroad were permitted the facility of overseas business acquisition through ADR/GDR stock swap under the automatic route subject to conditions that included adherence to FDI policy and the value limit for the transaction not to exceed US$ 100 million or 10 times the export earnings during the proceeding financial year.

To sum up, policies relating to portfolio investment in India have been substantially liberalised since the early 1990s.

Studies show that volatility of cross-border portfolio investment flows into India has been less than what has been experienced by other emerging market economies (EMEs). The stability in portfolio flows to India has been attributed to factors such as robust economic performance since early 1990s and relatively low level of co-movements between Indian and global stock prices. Empirical estimates indicate that FII flows are positively related to returns on BSE Sensex.

FII flows into India display seasonality, with inflows being significantly higher in the first four months of each calendar year. This could be due to global factors such as money flowing into the market at the start of the year from tax saving investments and from year-end bonuses. The pattern might also reflect improved domestic sentiment, since reforms are typically announced in the run-up to the end-February Union Budget.

Various supply and demand factors have made investing via institutions a rapidly growing sector in many developed countries. There is enhanced supply of funds from investors to institutions because of the aging of population, funded pension systems, and growing wealth. Institutions are also able to give better services and attractive returns because of ease of diversification, better corporate governance, liquidity, deregulation and fiscal incentives. Given this background, there is likely to be a large and growing demand for Indian stocks by FIIs.

The state of the domestic capital market is far more crucial to attracting foreign institutional investors than any special regime or dispensation. The focus, therefore, should be on improving the regulatory and supervisory framework governing the domestic capital markets and on technological modernisation of their operations. There has already been considerable progress in this regard, but it is still some distance away before the full range of financial instruments are introduced in India and innovations are expeditiously permitted.

Finally, there is no reason to expect that external investor confidence can be at variance with that of the domestic investor. Therefore, the precondition to attracting greater FII is the return of the domestic investor to the Indian capital markets.

Endnotes

1. While permitting foreign corporates/high net worth individuals in February 2000 to invest through SEBI registered FII/domestic fund managers, it was noted that there was a clear distinction between portfolio investment and FDI. The basic presumption is that FIIs are not interested in management control. To allay fears of management control being exercised by portfolio investors, it was noted that adequate safety nets were in force, for example: (a) transactions of business in securities on the stock exchanges

are only through stock brokers who have been granted a certificate by SEBI, (b) every transaction is settled through a custodian who is under obligation to report to SEBI and RBI for all transactions on a daily basis, (c) provisions of SEBI's Substantial Acquisition of Shares and Takeovers Regulations, 1997 and (d) monitoring of sectoral caps by RBI on a daily basis.

2. Government of India, Ministry of Finance, *Budget Speech of the Union Finance Minister,* 2011-12.

10

International Investment Position (IIP) and International Financial Integration (IFI) of South Asian Countries

10.1 Introduction

It is assumed that rise in cross-border investment flows add to the stock of foreign investment and can manifest its impact on the economies in different ways, including an increase in production and employment and ultimately helping the countries reach a higher level of growth. Post-1990s was the age of liberalization for most of the developing economies of the world whereby the countries experienced enormous flow of foreign capital. The rise in capital flows adds to the stock of foreign investment, commonly known as international investment position (IIP). International investment position (IIP), as defined by IMF's Balance of Payments and International Investment Positions Manual, 2008 (6th edition), "is a statistical statement that shows at a point of time, the values and composition of: (a) financial assets of residents of an economy that are claims on non residents and gold bullion held as reserve assets, and (b) liabilities of residents of an economy to non residents". IIP is a subset of national balance sheet of an economy.

International investment position consists of a two-sided entry, namely, assets comprising of value of foreign assets owned by a country's residents and, liability, comprising of value of a country's asset owned by foreigners. Foreign assets consist of: (a) foreign direct investment (FDI), (b) foreign portfolio investment (FPI), (c) foreign derivatives (FD), (d) other investments (OI), and (e) foreign reserves. Foreign liabilities encompass: (a) foreign direct investment (FDI), (b) foreign portfolio investment (FPI), (c) foreign derivatives (FD), and (d) other investments (OI).

Since international payments and investment positions claim a growing share of both corporate and national balance sheets, they also inevitably impact domestic financial variables and the level and composition of economic activity. IIP data is useful in understanding the financial structure from the gross assets and liabilities position angle. It is an important tool to judge whether a country is a net external creditor or a net external debtor (Shirai, 2009). Also, the volume-based measure of international financial integration (measured as summation of foreign assets and foreign liabilities as ratio of GDP) can be calculated from the IIP data (Lane and Milesi-Ferretti, 2003).

As stated by International Monetary Fund, in its *World Economic Outlook* (2014), increases in foreign holdings of domestic liabilities can raise the probability for different types of financial crises, including banking, currency, sovereign debt and sudden stops. Composition and size of external assets and liabilities through the IIP are used to detect possible risks arising from such capital reversal (Warsosemito, 2012).

Rise in cross-border assets trade, by removing restrictions on cross-border capital movements, makes countries more and more integrated. This helps countries to collect and distribute financial assets since these are required for fulfilling their financial and economic goals. Literature shows that a huge asset trade has been made during the globalized era. However, the concern is the pattern of debt and equity trade-off and the possible risks from that.

South Asia hosts nearly one-fourth of the world's population (23.6 percent in 2011), a real GDP of only about 3 percent (2.99 percent in 2011) of the world's real GDP (2005), and covers 3 percent of the world area. The region consists of heterogeneous group of countries with different languages, different ideologies different sizes and different level of developments. The member countries of South Asia include Afghanistan, Bangladesh,

Bhutan, India, Maldives, Nepal, Pakistan and Sri Lanka. These countries formed the South Asian Association for Regional Cooperation (SAARC) in 1985 with an aim to promote welfare economies, collective self-reliance and enhancing socio-cultural development in the region.

10.2 Review of Literature

The basic requirements of IFI were investigated by Von Furstenberg (1998) and he argued that IFI could not be assessed in isolation from a country's structure of financial institutions and markets. Martin and Rey (2001) focused on the importance of size of economies and transaction costs for trade flows in assets. Lane and Milesi-Ferretti (2001a) developed a dataset of the external wealth and found that trade openness is highly important in explaining the level of aggregate external liabilities for developing countries and also the ratio of equity to debt liabilities. Lane and Milesi-Ferretti (2002), opined that output per capita, public debt, and demographic variables have a major influence on the direction of international asset trade.

Lane and Milesi-Ferretti (2003) were the first who gave a detailed and comprehensive analysis of IFI using the panel data estimation with a sample of 18 OECD countries over the period 1978-2001. They examined the trends of IFI and identified goods trade and stock market capitalization as two key determinants of the growth in the scale of international balance sheets.

Gruic (2005) found that the level of development, domestic capital markets and lifting of restrictions on capital account, were the main determinants of international investment positions and integration of international capital market. Vo and Daly (2005a; 2005b) provided tests of other IFI concepts where they were related to the test of correlation among different macroeconomic variables.

Lane and Schmukler (2007) studied the international financial integration of China and India and identified domestic financial developments and policies such as financial liberalization, exchange rate policies, domestic financial sector policies and the impact of financial reform on savings and investment rates and concluded that they were essential in understanding the pattern of IFI.

Vo and Daly (2007) did an excellent work, taking a sample of 79 countries over a long period of time (1980-2003) and used advanced techniques for panel data estimation. They considered policy on capital controls, level of development, economic growth, institutional, legal and investment environment, trade openness, financial market developments, financial system and banking system, and tax policy as explanatory variables to determine IFI. Their analysis highlighted IMF capital control policy dummy, trade openness, domestic credit and economic growth as potential variables to explain the variation in the degree of IFI.

In another study by Fureceri, Guichard and Rusticeli (2012), it was found that the role of structural policies was considered as a key element. According to the paper, "certain kinds of structural policy reforms could help narrow global imbalances and modify the composition of international capital flows towards more stable and productive sources".

In their study by Arora and Ratnasiri (2014), the determinants of regional financial integration were used for the principal component analysis. The paper examined the current status of financial developments and financial cooperation in South Asia. The paper also tried to find the factors which are influencing regional financial integration. They found that the major determinants of regional financial integration were trade levels, income and political stability.

The aim of the paper was to find the determinants of IFI of South Asian countries. It was advancement over the previous researches since it considered some new variables and tried to examine whether these variables were significant or not in explaining IFI, while using the panel data estimation method.

10.3 Growth of Assets and Liabilities: Some Stylized Facts

In this section, we have presented some stylized facts showing the trends of IFI as well as total asset and liability positions and its components.

According to Lane and Milesi-Ferretti (2003), volume-based measure of international financial integration means:

$IFIGDP_{it} = (FA_{it} + FL_{it})/ GDP_{it}$

Where, *FA* and *FL* refer to the stocks of aggregate foreign assets and liabilities respectively.

Lane and Milesi-Ferretti (2003) also considered equity-based measure of IFI since international trade in debt instruments may be driven by special factors. The measure is:

$GEQGDP_{it} = (PEQA_{it}+FDIA_{it}+PEQL_{it}+FDIL_{it})/ GDP_{it}$

Where, *PEQ* stands for portfolio equity.

Figure 10.1 depicts that Bhutan had a falling trend in case of volume-based measure of IFI. Maldives showed a rising trend for both the measures. India showed an unstable trend of IFI in post-Crisis years in both the measurements. IFI was more of less stable in volume-based measure and rose in case of equity-based measure for South Asia as a whole.

Figure 10.1: Volume-Based and Equity-Based Measurement of IFI of Member Countries and South Asia as a Whole (in percent of GDP)

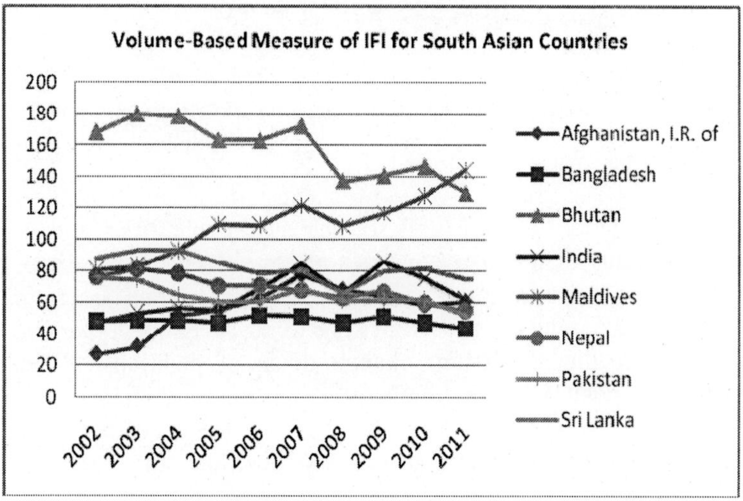

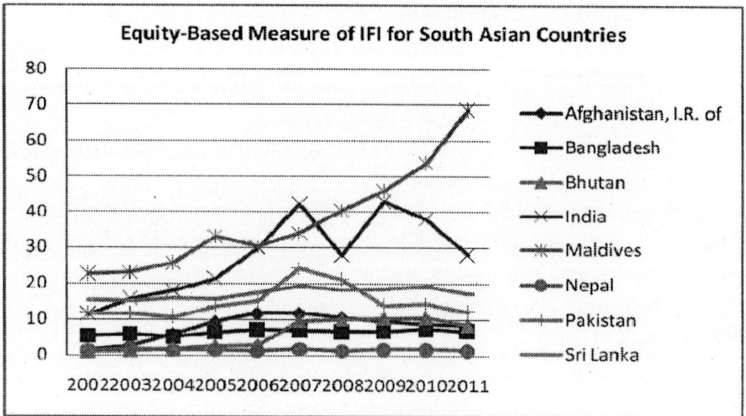

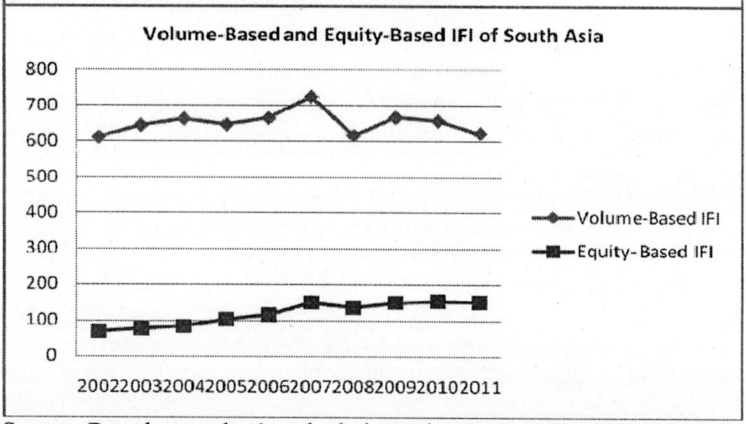

Source: Based on author's calculation using Lane and Milesi-Ferretti constructed database.

In Figure 10.2, we will see the assets, liabilities and its components of member countries of South Asia. We can see that there exists a sharp falling trend regards total assets of Bhutan. Afghanistan shows a rising trend of assets. Others do not have any significant change of asset positions. When liability positions are compared, we can see that except Maldives, which shows a sharp rising trend, there is no significant change in total liability positions of remaining countries.

Figure 10.2: Total Assets and Liabilities of Member Countries of South Asia

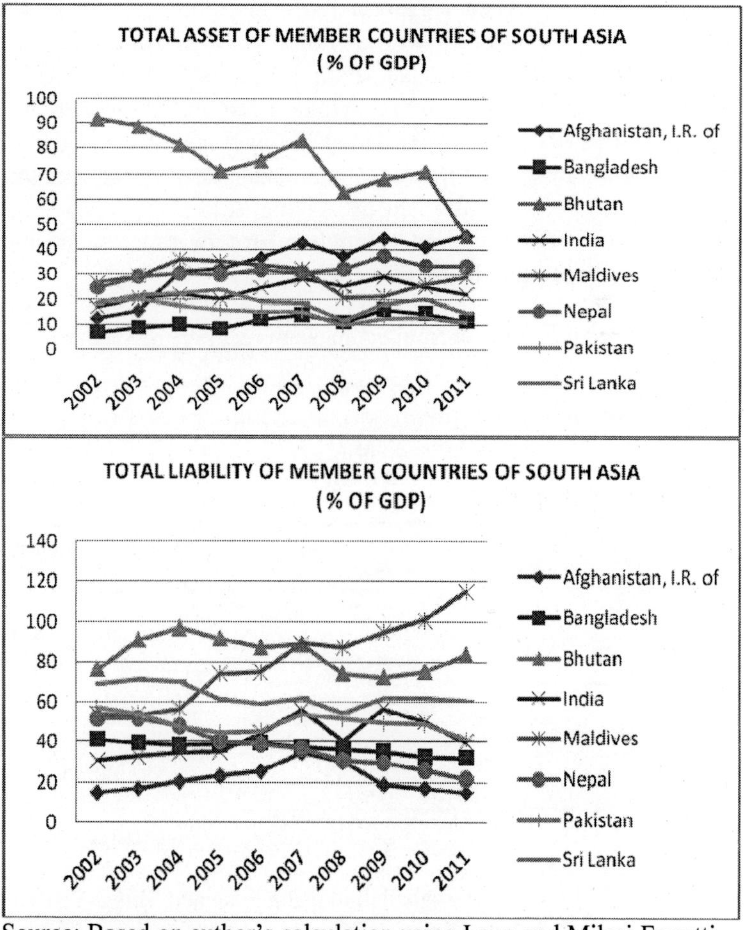

Source: Based on author's calculation using Lane and Milesi-Ferretti constructed database.

In Figure 10.3, NFL position of member countries has been depicted. Maldives has shown a sharp rising trend and contrarily, Nepal shows a falling trend. Others do not have any significant deviation. It needs to be mentioned here, that among the countries, only Afghanistan (for the whole period) and Nepal since 2009, had net assets position.

Table 10.1 presents growth rates of South Asia and its members. When asset growth is compared with South Asia, it is discernible that Bangladesh, India, Maldives and Nepal were close to the average. However, Afghanistan had 39.47 percent growth of assets which augmented the average. When we see the growth rate of liabilities, Bhutan had the highest growth rate of 24.6 percent followed by Afghanistan at 20.8 percent. These two countries showed higher growth rates than the average growth rate (17.83 percent).

Figure 10.3: NFA of South Asia as percentage of World

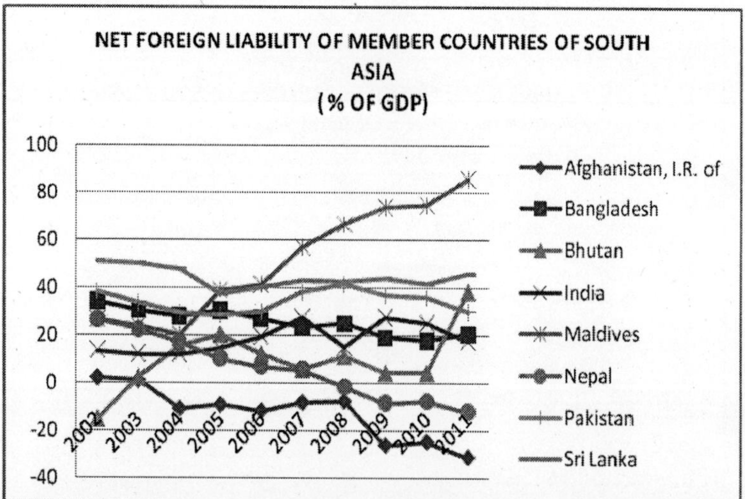

Source: Based on author's calculation using Lane and Milesi-Ferretti constructed database.

10.4 Conclusion

In this chapter, we studied the trends and determinants of IFI of South Asian countries. Stylized facts show that following both volume-based and equity-based measures of IFI, Maldives showed a significant rising trend and South Asia as a whole had a rising trend in equity-based measure. Our detailed analysis of assets and liabilities show that Maldives had a rising trend of foreign liabilities too. Generally, RA, DA and FDI were the important foreign investment asset components for the South Asian countries. In case of liabilities, DL, FDIL and FPEL were the important components. Among the member countries, India was the highest receiving or lending country. Also, NFL position of India as percentage of GDP was much better than the other five countries.

Table 10.1: Average Growth Rates of Total Assets and Liabilities of South Asian Countries during 1985-2011* (in percentage)

	Afghanistan	Bangladesh	Bhutan	India	Maldives
Assets	39.47	14.77	11.43	17.30	16.55
Liabilities	20.86	6.23	24.60	12.57	14.10

contd...

	Nepal	Pakistan	Sri Lanka	South Asia (Total)
Assets	16.16	11.92	9.29	18.44
Liabilities	8.04	7.54	9.14	17.83

*Due to unavailability of data, growth rate Afghanistan was calculated from 2002 to 2011. Growth rate of South Asia was also calculated for the same period (2002-2011).

Source: Based on author's calculation using Lane and Milesi-Ferretti constructed database.

For finding out the determinants of international financial integration, our study considered fifteen explanatory variables viz. lagged IFI, market size, domestic financial developments, trade openness, regulatory quality, exchange rate volatility, inflation volatility, globalization index, competitiveness index, crisis dummy, money and quasi money (M2), tax rate, infrastructure, general government final consumption expenditure and building of human resources. Empirical study reveals that crisis dummy, domestic financial developments, regulatory quality, inflation volatility, lagged IFI, infrastructure, money and quasi money (M2) and trade openness were significant in explaining the volume-based measure of international financial integration and variables such as domestic financial development, inflation volatility, exchange rate volatility lagged IFI, infrastructure, money and quasi money (M2) and trade openness were significant in explaining the equity-based measure of international financial integration. A detailed study of the economic conditions and policies of individual countries may be carried out for further clarification of the results.

11

Determinants of International Financial Integration (IFI) of 12 European Union (EU) Countries

11.1 Introduction

In this liberalised era, both flows and stock of foreign investment has shown a rising trend worldwide. Rise in outflows and inflows of foreign investment results in an increase in inward and outward stock of foreign investment. Since international financial integration is measured by stock of foreign investment assets as well as stock of liabilities, rise in foreign investment assets and liabilities ultimately raises international financial integration. Absolute measures of international financial integration show how much a country is integrated with the world capital market and other measures depict the composition, pointing towards the indication of degree of instability it may possibly have. A study of the determinants of international financial integration is necessary for understanding different economic variables that may invite different types of foreign capital—especially the volatile ones in large amount—in a country and in the process may lead to economic crisis.

In this chapter, for the period 1985 to 2011, we have chosen 12 European Union members. Most of the European Union (EU) members belong to the high income group. European Union members are very strong, powerful and their trade integration is higher compared to the other unions such as ASEAN and SAARC (Pal and Bhattacharya, 2012). Also, the literature shows that international financial integration of high income countries was higher compared to the middle income and low income group (Ghosh and Bhattacharya, 2016).

We have tried to find out the determinants of international financial integration of these 12 European Union members, using the co-integrating panel regressions.

11.2 Review of Literature

A limited number of studies pertaining to the determinants of international financial integration were found. Depending on the data, different studies applied different techniques and found several important factors affecting the degree and composition of international financial integration. According to Von Furstenberg (1998), a country's structure of financial institutions and markets affects its degree of IFI to a great extent. Martin and Rey (2001) found that the size of an economy and the transaction costs of asset trade are important factors in determining the IFI of a country. Lane and Milesi-Ferretti (2001a) developed a dataset of external wealth and using that dataset, they found that trade openness was highly important in explaining the level of aggregate external liabilities of developing countries and also the rise of the debt-equity liability ratio (Lane and Milesi-Ferretti 2001b).

Lane and Milesi-Ferretti (2002) provided an extensive analysis of net foreign asset position for 22 industrial and 38 developing countries for the period 1970-1998. They found the variables as non-stationary and hence used non-stationary panel estimation and vector error correction. Applying the dynamic ordinary least squares (DOLS), they found that output per capita, public debt and demographic variables, had a significant effect on the direction of international asset trade. The paper was a benchmark one for the analysis of international financial integration as it had considered a considerable number of countries and advanced panel techniques available at that point of time.

As we find, Lane and Milesi-Ferretti (2003) were probably the first who gave a detailed and comprehensive analysis of IFI using the panel data estimation with a sample of 18 OECD countries for the period 1978-2001. They examined the trends of IFI and identified goods trade and stock market capitalization as two key determinants for such trends. Gruic (2005) found that the level of economic development as well as development of the domestic capital market and absence of restrictions on capital account were the main determinants of international investment position and integration with the international capital market.

Lane and Schmukler (2007) found that domestic financial developments and policies attempting financial liberalization as well as exchange rate policies were important determinants of IFI. They showed that financial reforms affect IFI through its impact on domestic savings and investment rates.

Vo and Daly (2007) considered sample of 79 countries for the period 1980-2003 and used advanced techniques of panel data estimation. They considered policies on capital controls, level of development, economic growth, institutional, legal and investment environment, trade openness, financial market developments, financial system and banking system and tax policy as explanatory variables. They used panel ordinary least squares (OLS), two stage least squares (2SLS), and generalized method of moments (GMM) system methods. They found that IMF capital control policy dummy, trade openness, domestic credit and economic growth were the variables that explain the variation in the degree of IFI.

In their attempt to find out the determinants of international financial integration in the global business area, while considering fifteen international stock markets (G7 stock market and eight emerging markets) for the period 1988-2008, Arfaoui and Abaoub (2010), considered a large number of local (pull) and global (push) factors. As measures of international financial integration, they factored in total assets and total liabilities as well as FDI assets and liabilities.

The local factors included domestic economic growth, domestic inflation, trade openness, local investment, local tax policy, financial developments measured by market capitalization to GDP and domestic credit to GDP, gross dividend yields, domestic institutional and legal environment, indices of corruption perception and financial liberalization. The global factors included world interest rates, world industrial production and global growth opportunities. Applying the dynamic panel data estimation, Arellano and Bond (1991) found that socio-economic stability, trade openness, financial development and growth opportunities were important pull factors that drive international financial integration. World interest rates, world economic situation and world PER were found to be important push factors.

In another study, Fureceri et al. (2012) found that the structural policies were a key factor in determining the composition and nature of IFI. According to the paper, "certain kinds of structural policy reforms could help narrow global imbalances and modify the composition of international capital flows towards more stable and productive sources".

Garali and Othmani (2015) dealt with the determinants of international financial integration for Middle East and North African Countries (MENA). They considered control variables such as trade openness, level of development, financial market developments, inflation rate, fluctuations in exchange rate, financial crisis of 2008, and tax policy.

They took into account eight countries of the MENA region for the period 2006 to 2012. The paper found trade openness, exchange rate volatility and log GDP as significant variables to explain international financial integration in the MENA region. They also considered external debt as a measure of international financial integration.

Bhattacharya and Ghosh (2016) analysed the determinants of equity-based measures of international financial integration of South Asian countries for the period 2004 to 2011. Applying the panel GMM technique, they found that lagged value of equity-based measure of IFI, trade openness and globalization were significant in explaining the equity-based measure of international financial integration.

Thus, the important determinants of international financial

integration, as found in the existing literature, include domestic economic as well as financial developments, size of the economy, trade openness, institutional, legal and investment environment of an economy, inflation and exchange rate volatility, domestic credit availability, transaction costs involved with asset trade, tax and other structural policies, capital control policies and other reform measures. We have considered a subset of these factors in this book.

11.3 Concepts, Measures and Trends of International Financial Integration

There are several aspects of international financial integration such as international trade integration, financial market integration, and economic integration between different unions etc.

International financial integration is basically defined as a process by which a country integrates its financial capital market with the global financial capital market.

According to Lane and Milesi-Ferretti (2003), there are two measures of international financial integration, namely, volume-based measure and equity-based measure.

Also, there exist a number of methods to measure international financial integration like debt measures and measures with different combinations of components of total foreign assets and liabilities. However, in this chapter, we will concentrate only the following two measures of international financial integration.

Based on Lane and Milesi-Ferretti (2003), volume-based measure of international financial integration is calculated as:

$$IFIVB_{it} = (FA_{it} + FL_{it})*100/GDP_{it}$$

and, equity-based measure is calculated as:

$$IFIEQ_{it} = (PEQA_{it}+FDIA_{it}+PEQL_{it}+FDIL_{it})*100/GDP_{it}$$

Where, *FA* and *FL* refer to the stocks of aggregate foreign assets and liabilities respectively. PEQ stands for portfolio equity and FDI is denoted as foreign direct investment.

The period of study was selected from 1985 onwards. The

12 European Union members include Belgium, Denmark, France, Germany, Greece, Ireland, Italy, Luxembourg, Netherlands, Portugal, Spain and UK. Among the 12 countries, Portugal belonged to the upper middle income group and all other countries belonged to the high income group.

Average values of IFIVB and IFIEQ for the period 1985 to 2011 for 12 EU member economies are presented in Table 11.1. As is evident from the Table, amongst the group of 12 EU member countries, Luxembourg was an outlier, containing very high values for both the measures.

Accordingly, we have excluded Luxembourg while carrying out the trend analysis for the group as a whole.

Table 11.1: Average Values of IFIVB and IFIEQ of 12 EU Member Countries for the Period 1985 to 2011

Country Name	IFIVB	IFIEQ
Belgium	596.0195	199.9576
Denmark	280.768	82.17321
France	293.841	101.4947
Germany	231.0747	60.74461
Greece	146.8253	22.95237
Ireland	1220.399	419.4342
Italy	159.3809	43.21839
Luxembourg	17244.66	9695.028
Netherlands	518.3941	209.484
Portugal	248.3871	57.26624
Spain	182.8785	60.58992
United Kingdom	639.0421	141.8005

Source: Author's calculation based on Lane and Milesi-Ferretti database.

These trends of IFIVB and IFIEQ have also been presented in Figure 11.1. The gap between the two measures of IFI was rising, especially after 2000. In 2008, we see a sharp fall for both the curves. This may be due the effect of global financial crisis.

Figure 11.1: Trends of IFIVB and IFIEQ of 12 EU Member Countries for the Period 1985 to 2011

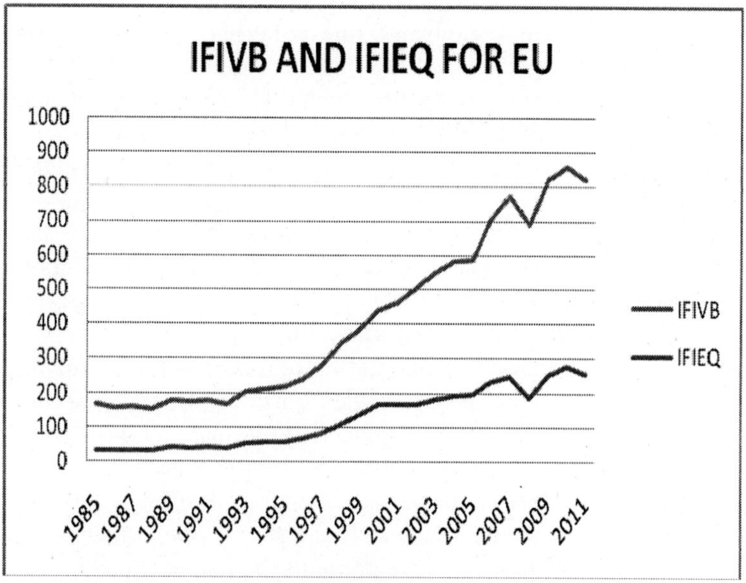

11.4 Summary and Conclusion

The nature of flows and hence of the stock, most times, differs across countries/country groups, thus giving rise to varied international investment positions or international financial integration of the countries. Although, a large number of studies have analyzed the nature and growth of international financial integration post-1990s, only a few studies have dealt with its determinants.

As suggested by the existing literature, there are a number of factors influencing the international financial integration of a country. In this chapter, we have investigated the macroeconomic determinants of international financial integration of 12 European Union member countries over the period from 1985 to 2011. We considered a number of economic factors including inflation volatility, exchange rate volatility, per capita GDP growth, lagged annual GDP growth rate, financial developments and trade openness as well as non-economic factors like restrictions on capital flows.

Data shows that exchange rate volatility, per capita GDP growth, and lagged annual GDP growth rate are stationary in nature and trade openness, financial developments and restrictions on capital flows and also dependent variables such as IFIVB and IFIEQ, are non-stationary in levels and stationary in first differenced form, i.e., integrated of order one or I(1). We ran the panel co-integration test with the I(1) variables to check whether long-run relationship between these variables exists or not and found that these variables are co-integrated and do have a long-run relationship.

We applied panel co-integrating regressions for estimating the long-run relationship. The co-integrating regression models, Pedroni Panel Fully Modified Ordinary Least Squares (FMOLS) and Dynamic Ordinary Least Squares (DOLS) revealed that trade openness, financial developments and restrictions were on expected lines, meaning that trade openness and financial developments had a positive impact and restrictions on capital flows had a negative impact on international financial integration.

For both the measures of IFI, variables trade openness and restrictions on capital flows were significant in case of FMOLS and only trade openness was significant in case of DOLS, in determining international financial integration of the European Union Members.

Bibliography

Bibliography

Acharya, A. and Prakash, A. (2013), "International Financial Integration, Capital Flows and Growth of Asian Economies", Reserve Bank of India Occasional Papers, 34 (1-2).

Agenor, P.R. (2003), "Benefits and Costs of International Financial Integration: Theory and Facts", *World Economy*, 26(8), 1089-1118.

Anderson, T.W. and Hsiao, C. (1981), "Estimation of Dynamic Models with Error Components", *Journal of the American Statistical Association* 76, 598-606.

Anderson, T.W. and Hsiao, C. (1982), "Formulation and Estimation of Dynamic Models Using Panel Data", *Journal of Econometrics,* 18, 47-82.

Arfaoui, M. and Abaoub, E. (2010), "On the Determinants of International Financial Integration in the Global Business Area", *Journal of Applied Economic Sciences*, 5, 3(13).

Arora, R.U. and Ratnasiri, S. (2014), "Financial Integration of South Asia: An Exploratory Study", *New Zealand Journal of Asian Studies*, 16(1), 39-60.

Bhattacharya, A. and Ghosh, A. (2014), "FDI and International Investment Position (IIP): A Case Study of India During 1999-2012", in 'Foreign Direct Investment in Retail Business: Challenges and Opportunities', (eds.) Jaydeb Bera and Rohini Nandan, Kolkata.

Bhattacharya, A. and Ghosh, A. (2016a), "Trend and Determinants of Equity Based Measure of International Financial Integration of South Asian Countries: A Panel GMM-IV Approach", seminar proceedings of the International Seminar on Contemporary Issues on Economic Development with Special Reference to Agriculture and Food Security, Department of Economics with Rural Development, Vidyasagar University, Midnapore, West Bengal, January 13-14.

Bhattacharya, A. and Ghosh, A. (2016b), "Short-term Determinants of International Financial Integration of Middle Income Countries", *International Journal of Research on Social and Natural Sciences,* 1(1), June.

Bhattacharya, A. (2019), "Economic Development and International Financial Integration: An Empirical Study of Selected Countries", unpublished Ph.D. thesis, University of Kalyani.

Bhattacharya, A., Ghosh, A. and Bhattacharya, S. (2015), "A Comparative Analysis of International Investment Position of Selected Developed and Developing Countries: An Indication of Capital Leveraging in the Globalised Era", in 'Financial Sector Reforms in Developing Economies', (eds.) Samir Ghosh, Abhijit Ghosh, Tarak Nath Sahu, Brajaballav Paul, and Rohini Nandan.

Blundell, R. and Bond, S. (1998), "Initial Conditions and Moment Restrictions in Dynamic Panel Data Models", *Journal of Econometrics*, 87(1), 115-143.

Boonstra, W. (2008), "National Savings and the International Investment Position: What Does the Current Account Tell Us",? *Zb. rad. Ekon. fak. Rij.*, Vol. 26, 9-40.

Breitung, J. (2000), "The Local Power of Some Unit Root Tests for Panel Data in Advances in Econometrics", in ed. (ed.) B.H. Baltagi, 'Non-stationary Panels, Panel Co-integration, and Dynamic Panels', 161-178.

Brewer, T. L. and Nollen, S. D. (2000), "Direct Investment and Portfolio Flows to Developing Countries", unpublished, The World Bank.

Brushko, L. and Hashimoto, Y. (2014), "The Role of Country Concentration in the International Portfolio Investment Positions for the European Union Members", IMF Working Paper WP/14/74.

Caprio, G. and Honohan, P. (1999), "Restoring Banking Stability: Beyond Supervised Capital Requirements", *Journal of Economic Perspectives*, 13, 43-64.

Chinn, M. and Ito, H. (2008), "A New Measure of Financial

Openness", *Journal of Comparative Policy Analysis*, 10 (3), 309-322.

Chuhan, P., Quiros, G.P. and Popper, H. (1996), "International Capital Flows: Do Short-Term Investment and Direct Investment Differ?", PRE Working Paper No. 1669, The World Bank.

Cyrus, T.L., Iscan, T.B. and Starky, S. (2006), "Investor Protection and International Investment Positions: An Empirical Analysis", *International Finance*, 9(2), 197-221.

Dadush, U., Dasgupta, D., and Ratha, D. (2000), "The Role of Short-term Debt in Recent Crises", *Finance and Development*, 37, 54-57.

Degre, C. and Reimers, H.E. (2005), "Healthcare Expenditures in OECD Countries: A Panel Unit Root and Co-integration Analysis", IZA Discussion Paper No. 1469.

Dickey, D.A. and Fuller, W.A. (1979), "Distribution of the Estimators for Autoregressive Time Series With a Unit Root", *Journal of the American Statistical Association*, 74 (366), 427-431.

Dumitrescu, E.I. and Hurlin, C. (2012), "Testing for Granger Non-causality in Heterogeneous Panels", *Economic Modelling*, 29, 1450-1460.

Engle, R.F. and Granger, C.W.J. (1987), "Co-Integration and Error Correction: Representation, Estimation and Testing", *Econometrica*, 55(2), 251-276.

Furceri, D. Guichard, S. and Rusticelli, E. (2012), "Medium-Term Determinants of International Investment Positions: The Role of Structural Policies", *Journal of International Commerce, Economics and Policy (JICEP),* World Scientific Publishing Co. Pte. Ltd., 3(02), 1250012-1-1.

Garali, W. and Othmani, S. (2015), "The Determinants of International Financial Integration in the MENA Area", *Procedia Economics and Finance,* 26, 535-541.

Ghosh, A. and Bhattacharya, A. (2016a), "Macroeconomic Determinants of International Financial Integration of High Income OECD Countries: A Panel Co-integration

Analysis", paper presented in the International Conference in Applied Economics, Macro and Empirical Finance (AMEF, 2016), Thessaloniki, Greece, University of Macadonia, May 6-7 May.

Gourinchas P.O. and Jeanne, O. (2007), "Capital Flows to Developing Countries: The Allocation Puzzle", NBER Working Paper No. 13602.

Gourinchas, P.O., Oscar, L. and Rodrigo, V. (2001), "Lending Booms: Latin America and the World", NBER Working Paper No. 8249.

Granger, C.W.J. (1969), "Investigating Causal Relations by Econometric Models and Cross-spectral Methods", *Econometrica*, 37(3), 424-438.

Grohe′, S.S. and Uribe, M. (2004), "International Macroeconomics", available at: www.columbia.edu/~mu 2166/UIM /notes.pdf.

Gruic,′ B. (2005), "Determinants of International Investment Position", Croatian National Bank, Zagreb, Croatia, available at: http://ssrn.com/abstract=2239269.

Ho, N.W. (2009), "Financial Integration: Concepts and Impacts", *Macao Monetary Research Bulletin*, 10, 69-84.

Im, K.S., Pesaran, M.H. and Shin, Y. (2003), "Testing for Unit Roots in Heterogeneous Panels", *Journal of Econometrics*, 115, 53-74.

International Monetary Fund (1993), "Balance of Payments Manual", 5th edition.

International Monetary Fund (2008), "Balance of Payments and International Investment Position Manual", 6th edition.

International Monetary Fund, "International Financial Statistics Yearbook", *various issues*.

Jackson K.J. (2012), "The United States as a Net Debtor Nation: Overview of the International Investment Position", Congressional Research Service, available at: www.crs.gov.

Kao, C. and Chiang, M. (2000), "On the Estimation and Inference of a Co-integrated Regression in Panel Data", *Advance in Econometrics,* 15, 179-222.

Kose, M.A., Prasad, E.S. and Terrones, M.E. (2006), "How Do Trade and Financial Integration Affect the Relationship Between Growth and Volatility?", *Journal of International Economics*, 69(1), 176-202.

Krugman, P. and Obstfeld, R. (2009), "International Economics Theory and Policy", Pearson.

Lane, P.R. and Milesi-Ferretti, G.M. (2000), "External Capital Structure: Theory and Evidence", IMF Working Paper. WP/00/152.

Lane, P.R. and Milesi-Ferretti, G.M. (2001), "The External Wealth of Nations: Measures of Foreign Assets and Liabilities for Industrial and Developing Countries", *Journal of International Economics*, 55, 263-294.

Lane, P.R. and Milesi-Ferretti, G.M. (2002), "Long-Term Capital Movements", NBER Macroeconomics Annual 2001, Vol. 16, (eds.) Ben S. Bernanke and Kenneth Rogoff, MIT Press.

Lane, P.R. and Milesi-Ferretti, G.M. (2003), "International Financial Integration", IMF Staff Paper, Vol. 50, Special Issue.

Lane, P.R. and Milesi-Ferretti, G.M. (2003b), "International Investment Patterns", mimeo, Trinity College Dublin and International Monetary Fund.

Lane, P.R. and Milesi-Ferretti, G.M. (2004a), "International Investment Patterns", IIIS Discussion Paper No. 24.

Lane, P.R. and Milesi-Ferretti, G.M. (2004b), "The Transfer Problem Revisited: Net Foreign Assets and Real Exchange Rates", *Review of Economics and Statistics*, LXXXVI(4).

Lane, P.R. and Milesi-Ferretti, G.M. (2007), "The External Wealth of Nations Mark II: Revised and Extended Estimates of Foreign Assets and Liabilities, 1970-2004", *Journal of International Economics,* 73(2), 223-250.

Lane, P.R. and Milesi-Ferretti, G.M. (2008), "The Drivers of

Financial Globalization", *American Economic Review*, 98(2), 327-332.

Lane, P.R. and Milesi-Ferretti, G.M. (2010), "The Cross-Country Incidence of the Global Crisis", IMF Working Paper No. WP/10/171.

Lane, P.R. (2000), "International Investment Positions: A Cross-Sectional Analysis", *Journal of International Money and Finance*, 19(4), 513-534.

Lane, P.R. (2010), "International Financial Integration and the External Positions of Euro Area Countries", OECD Economics Department Working Papers No. 830.

Levchenko, A.A. and Mauro, P. (2007), "Do Some Forms of Financial Flows Help Protect from Sudden Stops?", *World Bank Economic Review*, 21(3), 389-411.

Levin, A., Lin, C.F. and Chu, C.S.J. (2002), "Unit Root Tests in Panel Data: Asymptotic and Finite Sample Properties", *Journal of Econometrics,* 108(1), 1-24.

Martin, P. and Rey, H. (2001), "Financial Super-Markets: Size Matters for Asset Trade", National Bureau of Economic Research Working Paper No. 8476.

Obstfeld, M. and Rogoff, K. (2000), "The Six Major Puzzles in International Macroeconomics: Is There a Common Cause?", NBER Working Paper Series, 7777.

Offermanns, C. and Pramor, M. (2007), "The CFS International Capital Flow Database: A User's Guide", CFS Working Paper No. 2007/24, Centre for Financial Studies, Goethe University, Frankfurt.

Pedroni, P. (1999), "Critical Values for Co-integration Tests in Heterogeneous Panels with Multiple Regressors", *Oxford Bulletin of Economics and Statistics*, 61(0), 653-670.

Pedroni, P. (2000), "Fully Modified OLS for Heterogeneous Co-integrated Panels", in Baltagi, T.B. Fomby and R.C. Hill (eds.), 'Non-stationary Panels, Panels Co-integration, and Dynamic Panels: Advances in Econometrics'.

Pedroni, P. (2004), "Panel Co-integration: Asymptotic and Finite Sample Properties of Pooled Time Series Tests with an Application to the PPP Hypothesis", *Econometric Theory*, Cambridge University Press, 20(3), 597-625.

Phillips, P.C.B. and Perron, P. (1988), "Testing for a Unit Root in Time Series Regression", *Biometrika*, 75(2), 335-346.

Pistelli, A., Selaive, J. and Rodrigo Valdés, O. (2008), "Stocks, Flows, and Valuation Effects of Foreign Assets and Liabilities: Do They Matter?", in Kevin Cowan, Sebastián Edwards, Rodrigo O. Valdés and Norman Loayza (eds.), 'Current Account and External Financing', Central Bank of Chile, 237-277.

Prusty, R., Tanna J.J. and Denis L. (2013), "External Asset-Liability Position: An Emerging Facet of India's Investment Abroad, Contemporary Issues of Tourism, Banking and Education", Manglam Publishers and Distributors, New Delhi.

Reinhart C.M. and Reinhart V.R. (2008), "Capital Flow Bonanzas: An Encompassing View of the Past and Present", NBER Working Paper No. 14321.

Saikkonen, P. (1991), "Asymptotically Efficient Estimation of Co-integration Regressions", *Econometric Theory*, 7, 1-21.

Sarno, L. and Taylor, M. P. (1999), "Hot Money, Accounting Labels and the Permanence of Capital Flows to Developing Countries: An Empirical Investigation", *Journal of Development Economics*, 59, 337-364.

Shirai S. (2009), "Cross-border Investment and the Global Financial Crisis in the Asia- Pacific Region", UNESCAP Working Paper No. WP/09/04.

The Reserve Bank of India (2007), "Report on Currency and Finance", Mumbai: RBI.

Vo, X.V. and Daly, K.J. (2007), "The Determinants of International Financial Integration", *Global Finance Journal Elsevier*, 18(2), 228-250.

Von Furstenberg, G.M. (1998), "From Worldwide Capital Mobility to International Financial Integration: A Review Essay", *Open Economies Review*, 9, 53-89.

Warsosemito, R. (2012), "The International Investment

Position of Suriname", presented at the 44th Annual Monetary Studies Conference, Paramaribo, Suriname.

World Economic Outlook (2014), "International Monetary Fund", available at: www.imf.org.

Index

Index